THE AGE
OF THE SAINTS
IN THE EARLY
CELTIC CHURCH

ISBN 1 86143 031 0

Facsimile reprint
LLANERCH PUBLISHERS,
Felinfach.

These lectures were delivered in 1960 as part of the Riddell Memorial Lecture series. The lectures, which were founded in 1928, are given bi-ennially in the University of Newcastle upon Tyne, England.

The Age of the Saints
in the
Early Celtic Church

The Riddell Memorial Lectures
Thirty-second Series
delivered at King's College in the
University of Durham
on 22, 23, and 24 March 1960

BY

NORA K. CHADWICK

ISBN 1 86143 031 0

Facsimile reprint
LLANERCH PUBLISHERS,
Felinfach.

IN DESERTO PEREGRINANTIBUS
DEDICAVI

CONTENTS

PREFACE

I AM grateful to the Trustees of the Riddell Memorial Foundation in the University of Durham for inviting me to give these lectures.

The Age of the Saints in the Celtic Church is not only a period of especial beauty in early Christianity, but it also lies at the foundation of all our studies of Celtic history, since we owe to it most of our earliest written records of the early Celtic countries. It is for these reasons that I have chosen to concentrate on the literary rather than on the theological aspect of the Age of the Saints. The contemplation of their austerity, their unworldliness, and their spiritual happiness is an inspiration to our present age.

I wish to express my thanks to Dr. Owen Chadwick, Dixie Professor of Ecclesiastical History in Cambridge, and to Dr. Bertram Colgrave, Reader Emeritus in the University of Durham, for their kindness in reading my manuscript, and also for their encouragement and for a number of criticisms and suggestions. They are, however, in no sense responsible for the views which I have expressed.

I should also wish to thank Dr. Jocelyn Hillgarth of the Warburg Institute for much kindness, especially for bringing to my notice the references acknowledged in my footnotes, and also for permission to quote from one of his forthcoming studies.

My long and delightful friendship with Dr. Eleanor Duckett, Litt.D., Professor Emeritus of Smith College, Northampton, Massachusetts, whose learning in these fields far surpasses my own, has been a constant stimulus to me for many years.

My most grateful thanks are due to the Reverend Derwas J. Chitty, whose Birkbeck Lectures delivered in Cambridge in 1959 on Egyptian and Palestinian Monasticism under the Christian Empire first suggested to me the present study, and who generously placed the manuscript of his lectures at my disposal.

I am grateful to Messrs. Constable for permission to quote the translations of Dr. Kuno Meyer from his *Ancient Irish Poetry* on pages 160-166.

NORA K. CHADWICK

Newnham College, Cambridge
September 1960

I am glad to have the opportunity, afforded by this reprint, of thanking the University of Durham for undertaking the publication of these lectures, and the Staff of the Oxford University Press for the care and help which they have bestowed on the production. My warm thanks are due to Professor D. A. Binchy of the Institute for Advanced Studies, Dublin, for a number of corrections to my original version of this edition. I need hardly add that I alone am responsible for any errors which may still remain.

Cambridge, 1963   N.K.C.

I

THE EARLY CHURCH
IN THE BRITISH ISLES, AND THE
CONTINENTAL AND EASTERN
BACKGROUND

THE title and purpose of the Foundation under which I
have the honour to speak permits me at the outset to say
why I have chosen the Celtic Church as a subject which
still has a value for the development of modern thought.
For the proud continental folk of the period of the Celtic
Church spoke of our islands as 'on the edge of the habitable globe'. And St. Columba, the greatest saint of the
Celtic Church, is believed to have died in Iona in 597,
the very year in which St. Augustine arrived in Kent,
to inaugurate a different Order and discipline in our
country, one which had its headquarters and its organization in Rome. Before a century had passed the end of
the Celtic Church was already in sight. In 731, when
the Venerable Bede wrote the closing words of his *Ecclesiastical History*, he rested happy in the reflection that
all the countries of Britain and Ireland, with the exception of the Welsh, had forsaken their former separatism
and accepted the Roman obedience. The Celtic Church
had passed like a dream in the night. For Bede the sun
shone on a new day. Yet despite his loyalty and devotion to the Roman Church, Bede is himself in a large
measure a product of the Celtic Church. His gentleness,
his unworldliness, his idealism, his love of stories of fantastic asceticism, spring from his boyhood's memories

of the Northumbria created by St. Aidan and St. Cuthbert and the early Church of Lindisfarne.

What then do we mean by the Celtic Church? Wherein does it differ from the Church of St. Patrick, which claims to have preceded it in Ireland, and which eventually superseded it? Nearly a millennium and a half has passed since it flourished, and it may well seem a far-off and fleeting memory, too remote from our troubled world to have a message for us today. Shall I confess the truth? I have chosen it because of its lasting beauty. The Celtic Church of the Age of the Saints, as we see it in their gentle way of life, their austere monastic settlements and their island retreats, the personalities of their saints, and the traditions of their poetry, expresses the Christian ideal with a sanctity and a sweetness which have never been surpassed, and perhaps only equalled by the ascetics of the Eastern deserts. I take courage in my choice of subject from the opening sentence of the Reverend Mr. Chitty's Birkbeck lectures on the Saints of the Eastern Deserts, delivered in Cambridge in 1959, in which he told us that he had decided to lecture on this subject because 'the saints and the monasteries of the desert have a relevance to our problems and outlook in this present age'.

Bede tells us that when King Edwin was debating with his nobles of Northumbria in 627 as to whether they should accept Christianity, an unnamed member of the king's council made a memorable speech. It is deservedly Bede's best-known piece of writing, but I beg you to forgive me for once again quoting it here because it expresses my hope that the Age of the Saints in the Celtic Church is a subject which falls within the purpose of the Riddell Foundation.

The present life of man, O King, seems to me, in comparison with that time which is unknown to us, like the swift flight of a sparrow through the room in which you sit at supper in winter round the fire, while the wind is howling and the snow is drifting without. It passes swiftly in at one door and out through another, feeling for the moment the warmth and shelter of your palace; but it flies from winter to winter and swiftly escapes from our sight. Even such is our life here, and if anyone can tell us certainly what lies beyond it, we shall do wisely to follow his teaching.

The scope of the various shades of meaning of the word *sanctus*, 'saint', is extremely wide. From the earliest times it has been used in both a technical and a vague connotation. Undoubtedly its earliest general sense was 'holy' (Greek ἅγιος); but its usage has at all times been understood as equally appropriate, on the one hand to a special form of holiness having the definite sanction of Christian ecclesiastical authority, and on the other to a quality vaguely conceived as appropriate to a special class of people merely by a consensus of popular opinions. Within these wide applications the word has been restricted at various times to a specialized usage. In the title which I have chosen for my course the word saints, as we understand the term, is far removed from its earliest usage.[1]

The 'Age of the Saints' denotes a definite historical period when the conception and terminology have undergone various transformations, or rather specializations of meaning, and when we have in mind a defined age and conception of sanctity quite different from, let us say, the Age of the Apostles, or the Martyrs, or

[1] For an analysis of the history and usages of the word reference may be made to H. Delehaye, *Sanctus* (Bruxelles, 1927); see especially pp. 24 ff., 32, 38, 55, 58.

the Confessors. The 'Age of the Saints' is a special
period in the history of the Western Church, especially
the Celtic Church, and it carries with it the implication
that at this time the Church was characterized by the
prevalence of 'saints'. It will be our task to examine the
special features of this period, and the characteristics of
its ecclesiastics or 'saints'.

The sanctity and devotion of the 'religious' of the
early monastic institutions may be assumed, and also
their public works and their ministrations to the sur-
rounding peoples; but it is not these things that I want
to stress here. I want to make for them a different claim.
Fundamentally what gave them their power, and what
constitutes our greatest debt to these dedicated Christian religious, the *sancti*, is that they inaugurated an
organization of the attitude of enlightenment. The 'Age
of the Saints' is the end of the 'Heroic Age' whenever
and wherever it prevails, the great step forward in the
history of civilization when the fact comes to be widely
accepted that the mind can effect more than military
strength. Enlightenment itself involves a graded form
of specialization. Further, the scholar and the ascetic
may follow different disciplines. Often they do; but
broadly speaking the change from the 'Heroic Age' to
the 'Age of the Saints', this age of enlightenment, is the
substitution of the pen for the sword. It comes about
with the introduction and widespread use of writing,
bringing education in its train. In the Western Church
the word *sanctus*, despite its original meaning of 'holy',
is generally, indeed primarily, used of a man in Orders,
and this carries with it the inevitable meaning of an
'educated', a 'literate' man, not necessarily a man de-
serving special veneration in virtue of his individual

merits, certainly not necessarily a 'saint' in any sense. Throughout the early centuries of Christianity in western Europe the *sancti* were the only educated class.

The 'Age of the Saints' may be said to include the period from the late fifth to the late seventh century. At this period, and throughout the early Middle Ages, the word 'saint' (*sanctus*) did not, in usage, necessarily denote more than an ecclesiastic, and so, by implication, an educated man. The first writer who uses the term as a special characteristic of Ireland is Marianus Scotus who in the late eleventh century writes in his chronicle, s.a. 674, 'Hibernia insula Scotorum sanctis viris plena habetur.'[1] He himself was one of the many Irish scholars working in continental communities, and in his use of the word *sanctus*, as in theirs, and indeed in the most widespread usage of everyday speech, the word had long ago become restricted to members of an ecclesiastical community of whatever kind, and so literate. It is their literate and literary aspects that I propose to study here.

In Bede's *History* the conversion of Northumbria under King Edwin is effected by St. Paulinus from Canterbury; but after the brief lapse into heathenism following Edwin's death, when the Christian King Oswald came to the throne in 633, it was not to Canterbury that he sent for ecclesiastics, but 'to the Scottish authorities'[2] from whom he and his companions had received baptism while in exile. It was from Iona, therefore, the foundation of St. Columba, and the head of the greatest organization in the Celtic Church in the sixth and seventh centuries, that Northumbria received the form of Christianity which belonged to Celtic lands

---

[1] Haddan and Stubbs, *Councils*, II. ii. 283.
[2] 'Misit ad majores natu Scottorum.' *H.E.* iii. 3.

in the Age of the Saints. For nearly forty years Celtic monks from the island sanctuary of Iona and its daughter foundations ministered to the Saxon kingdom of Northumbria from the island sanctuary of Lindisfarne.

Less than forty years later King Oswiu reversed the policy of Oswald. At a synod held at Whitby in 663 the issue was contested between the two Churches, the Roman and the Columban, and it turned on the question of the correct dating of the Easter festival, though the Celtic tonsure was also debated. The scene of the council as Bede reports it is not unlike Edwin's council of 627. A debate took place between Colmán the bishop of Lindisfarne, who spoke for the Celtic Church, and Wilfrid of the church of Ripon, who spoke for the Roman. Colmán and his followers retired defeated. Leaving his island church and monastery on Lindisfarne, and taking with him his Celtic followers, as well as about thirty Saxons whom he had trained, he made his way first to Iona, and then on to the island of Inishbófin off the remote west coast of Mayo. Their departure and the official abandonment of the Celtic Church in Northumbria are made the occasion by Bede for a picture of the Celtic Order which was passing for ever, and in this picture we can hardly fail to see Bede's own love for those old days which had come to an end almost in his own lifetime. The monks of Lindisfarne had, he tells us, very few buildings except the church, such was their poverty; and they had no property except their cattle, for any money given to them by the rich they immediately gave away to the poor. When the king came to pray in their church he brought with him only five or six retainers, and if they stayed for a meal they were fed only on the simple daily food of the brethren—

'for the whole care of those teachers was to serve God, not the world; to care for the soul, not the stomach'.

This vignette of a little Celtic community on the eve of their dispersion for ever may be set beside Bede's portrait of Aidan, their former bishop, which is a worthy eulogy and a requiem, the more so since it comes from one who is a strong opponent. It is our finest full-length portrait of a Celtic saint. Aidan, he tells us, had no possessions except his church and a few fields round it; but he used to travel about with the king to his country seats, where he had a church and a lodging, and these he used to make his temporary centres from which to go through the country round about preaching. Bede hated Aidan's views on the Easter dating with a seriousness which strikes us as strangely excessive today. Yet despite this he saw him as one who cultivated peace and love, purity and humility; as one who was above anger and greed, and who despised pride and conceit; as one diligent in prayer; courageous in checking the proud and powerful; tender to the sick and poor; and he adds: 'To sum up in brief what I have heard from those who knew him, he took pains never to neglect anything that he had learned from the writings of the apostles and prophets, and he set himself to carry them out with all his powers.'

In Aidan, Cuthbert, and surely in Bede himself we have the spirit which inspired the Celtic Church.

What fundamentally is the difference between these two Churches—the Celtic Church of Northumbria founded from Iona and the Church of Canterbury founded directly from Rome? What was the nature of the earliest Celtic Church in the West? What was the nature of the Roman Church in the West? What movements in the Continental Church were influencing the Christianity in our islands? In the microcosm of our islands we can watch two forms of Christian discipline transforming our people into a Christian community by methods which appear very diverse. To get the problem into focus it will be helpful to view it against the contemporary background, first of Gaul and western Europe, and then in comparison with the hermits and little communities or *lavrae* of the east Mediterranean area and the Syrian desert.

When we turn from our own islands to the Continent we find in the fourth and fifth centuries a struggle going on between two ideals. This struggle has much in common with the struggle between the ideals of the Celtic and the Roman Church in our islands in the following period. The fifth century in western Europe is one of the most interesting, if not the most important, in the history of thought. In the midst of the break-up of Roman authority, and the overwhelming tide of the Barbarian invasion, the Classical traditions and Classical literature still continued to exist as a living culture, and the Latin writers of Gaul speak to us very much like people of our own generation. No concessions are needed to establish a complete understanding. We share their critical judgements, their logical reasoning, their sense of proportion and detachment, their realistic attitude, and above all—the supreme test—their sense of humour. All this is because our educational system is virtually identical, and based on a Classical training.

In Gaul we can trace the development of the prevalent form of Church government where it had developed on the lines of the Roman administrative system.[1]

___

[1] For a summary statement of metropolitan sees, and of provincial

The Gaulish Church was essentially an urban Church, based on ancient legal and administrative precedent. The bishop had his see, his *sedes*, in the cities which were the ancient administrative centres of the province. This was in all probability the original form of church organization in the Province of Roman Britain also, with which St. Patrick would be familiar. Christian worship was a normal part of the national life in Gaul, of the routine organization of their Christian Church, and of their quiet and balanced lives before the Barbarian invasions. We see the grand old man Ausonius duly attending morning prayers in his private chapel, till, as he quaintly tells us, 'God has been prayed to enough'. We are privileged to look over the shoulder of Sidonius, bishop of Auvergne, as he writes to fellow bishops, consulting them on the qualifications of candidates for a vacant bishopric, and we note that a wife who belongs to an episcopal family of long standing is held to be an important asset.

At precisely this time, however, during the fourth and fifth centuries, with astonishing rapidity, a new light, born in the East, broke in upon this well-ordered if somewhat complacent and finite order of thought. The mysticism of the ancient East was penetrating to the West, combined with the severe intellectual thought of the Greek Church, and disciplined into a coherent penitential system by the ascetics of the Egyptian and Syrian deserts. This mysticism was introducing a new system of values and a cleavage in the spiritual life of

ecclesiastical administration at the end of the fourth century, see J. R. Palanque and P. de Labriolle, *The Church in the Christian Roman Empire*, ii (London, 1952), pp. 600 ff.; and especially pp. 634 ff., and the references there cited.

the West. It brought with it the responsibility of a deliberate choice. The Christian could follow the old path of a good life in the world, or a total dedication of himself to the spiritual life. With Rome crumbling, and her social institutions breaking down, Gaul overrun by military barbarian heroic bands and their followers, the good life in the world was that of practical service to the State, and above all military service. The new alternative offered by the spiritual ideal was a solitary life separated from the world and devoted to God by a system of ascetic discipline directed towards the goal of spiritual contemplation. Obviously the second alternative necessitated withdrawal from practical life, and so the monastic ideal entering western Europe initiated a new institution within the Church itself, never displacing the existing system, but encroaching on it and disturbing it. The choice of these alternatives necessitated a fresh adjustment in the life of every Christian, difficult to make. We have not succeeded even yet.

The military position of Europe in the fifth century, the Empire falling and the barbarians overrunning Europe, made the choice a particularly difficult one. Faustus of Riez felt the urgent necessity of impressing on the monks of the new monastery of Lérins the necessity of keeping always before them the realization that they themselves were combatants, though their battle was a spiritual one. Lérins, the new island monastery in the Mediterranean off the coast of Cannes, is a *castra*, an armed camp, and its ranks are the soldiers who have come, not for a lethargic peace, but for the sword of the spirit:

It is not [he preaches to them in one of his sermons] for quiet and security that we have formed a community in this monastery, but for a struggle and a conflict. We have met here for a contest, we have embarked on a war against our sins. For it is our sins that are our foes. . . . Our vigilance must be constantly on the alert, for this conflict will be without ending. There can be no treaty with this foe. . . . This struggle on which we are engaged is full of hardship, full of danger, for it is the struggle of man against himself, and will not end save with the life of man. For this purpose, therefore, have we gathered together to this tranquil retreat, this spiritual camp—that we may, day after day, wage an unwearying contest against our passions.[1]

I have touched on the Christian Church in Gaul and on the introduction of mysticism and monasticism from the East in the fourth century because our sources for the early years of the Celtic Church are few, and for the most part comparatively late. For any just understanding of the history of the Celtic Church in our own country it is essential that we should have some clear idea of the contemporary background. It is commonly assumed that Christianity first reached Britain from Gaul, and that Ireland was converted from Britain. For this last belief we have the authority of the writings believed to be the work of St. Patrick, as well as those of his early biographers. It has also been held[2] that certain words found in the earliest Irish ritual had reached Ireland, not in their original Latin form, but modified by transmission through a British (doubtless Welsh) milieu;[3] and we

---

[1] *Sermo*, xxiii (*Ad Monachos*, i), edited by A. Engelbrecht, *Fausti Reiensis Opera* (Vienna, 1891), pp. 315 ff.

[2] Zimmer, McNeill, Jackson. Cf. K. H. Jackson, *Language and History in Early Britain* (Edinburgh, 1953), ch. 4, and particularly pp. 133 f.

[3] The first (*Cothriche*) group are held to have been introduced by St. Patrick and therefore small in number because his Church was small;

shall see that certain later Irish documents, such as the *Catalogus Sanctorum* (cf. p. 71 below), claim to support this transmission. The Irish annals state that St. Patrick's mission to Ireland took place in the fifth century. But the form of the Church associated with St. Patrick has little in common with the Celtic Church as we find this flourishing in all the Celtic countries in the following century. What is the relationship between these two Churches?

We have no records of the actual conversion of Britain to Christianity, or of missionary enterprise during the Roman Occupation, but Tertullian, writing from Carthage in North Africa *c.* A.D. 200, seems to have had some knowledge of conditions in Britain, for in enumerating a bare list of the peoples who believe in Christ he adds: 'Also places in Britain, which, though inaccessible to the Romans, have yielded to Christ.'[1]

And the statement of Origen (*c.* 240)—that many of the Britons have not yet heard the Gospel—confirms this.[2] Elsewhere he alludes to the Christian faith as a unifying force among the Britons.[3] Strangely enough Gildas has no tradition of the introduction of Christianity; but references by Constantius in the fifth century, by Gildas in the sixth, and by Bede early in the eighth to the martyrdom of St. Alban and two other Christians are believed to be derived from early *passiones* commemorating the martyrdoms which probably took

the second much bigger (*Pádraig*) group in the sixth century, with full British influence on Irish monasticism.

[1] *Adversus Judæos*, cap. 7: 'Britannorum inaccessa Romanis loca Christo vero subdita.'

[2] *Homil.* xxviii *in Matt.* xxiv, *sec. Vet. Interpr.*

[3] *Homil.* iv *in Ezek. Hieron. interpr.*: 'Quando enim terra Britanniae ante adventum Christi in unius dei consensit religionem?'

place in Britain between 250 and 260.[1] Moreover we
have evidence for the Christian life both in archaeological remains[2] and in the Christian funerary inscriptions which form a continuous series following on from
those of the heathen Roman type. These are to be found
more especially—though not exclusively—in the western
coastal areas of Britain, and while they testify to a continuous tradition with the Roman funerary inscriptions,
they share in the range of proper names which became
fashionable in Gaul in the fifth century, indicating
that sea-borne traffic with the Continent continued un-
broken at this time.[3]

Morever it seems probable on the whole that British
early Christianity had had a continuous history.[4] Although in the fourth century Saxon raids were already
making the short sea-route across the Straits of Dover
difficult and dangerous, this route was patrolled by a
Roman fleet,[5] and throughout the century it is clear, not
only that the church organization was preserved, at
least in eastern Britain, but also that Britons took an
active part in contemporary continental thought in
ecclesiastical matters. Eusebius[6] has preserved for us the

[1] W. Levison, 'St. Alban and St. Alban's', *Antiquity*, xv (1941).
[2] See J. M. C. Toynbee, 'Christianity in Roman Britain', *Journal of the Archaeological Association*, series 3, xvi (1953). The most important of these archaeological remains is the Lullingstone Villa in Kent, of which the wall paintings, recovered in 1949, suggest a Christian private chapel in the second half of the fourth century.
[3] For the corpus of these inscriptions, see V. E. Nash-Williams, *The Early Christian Monuments of Wales* (Cardiff, 1950); and R. A. S. Macalister, *Corpus Inscriptionum Insularum Celticarum* (Dublin, 1945-9).
[4] For a general account, the work of Hugh Williams, *Christianity in Early Britain* (Oxford, 1912) is still valuable.
[5] See D. Atkinson, 'Classis Britannica' in *Historical Essays in Honour of James Tait* (Manchester, 1933), pp. 1 ff.; C. J. Starr, *The Roman Imperial Navy* (Cornell University Press, Ithaca, 1941).
[6] *Hist. Eccles.* X. v.

text of a letter sent by the Emperor Constantine summoning the bishops of western Europe to a conference at Arles in 314. The names are also recorded of three British bishops who were present at the Council, from York, London, and perhaps Lincoln, but more probably Colchester, the last-named being attended by a priest and a deacon[1]—representing in fact the three senior orders of the church hierarchy. Further we again find three British bishops, probably from the same sees, taking a prominent place in the Synod of Rimini summoned by Constantine in 359 in his efforts to formulate a unity of belief acceptable to the whole Church. Moreover the part taken by the British bishops in continental councils is something more than a mere show of hands. The writings of both Hilary of Poitiers and St. Athanasius, Patriarch of Alexandria, state repeatedly that they count the Britons among their supporters in combating Arianism.

In the following century Britain gained a far greater prominence by the part which she played in regard to the Pelagian heresy which spread rapidly over Europe in the fifth century and stimulated some of the most important controversial literature of the time, including many of the writings of St. Augustine of Hippo and of the School of Marseilles. Among the latter was one of the most active opponents of the heresy, Prosper of Aquitaine. Pelagius, the heresiarch, was accused by his opponents of holding the view that denied original sin, and claiming that man can avoid sin by the power of the 'free-will without the aid of divine Grace' and that infants who die unbaptized are not necessarily debarred

[1] Professor Toynbee has pointed out that the third bishop, Adelphius, must therefore have been the most important (op. cit., p. 4).

from the Beatific Vision hereafter.[1] The controversy came to be commonly referred to briefly as that of 'Grace' and 'Free-will'. The views of Pelagius are most fully expressed in his Commentary on St. Paul's Epistles and in his letters; but, though some new fragments have recently come to light, most of his works have perished, and his views are chiefly known to us through the works of his opponents. It is often difficult, therefore, to ascertain the precise nature of the views which he actually held. Pelagius himself was a Celt from our islands by birth,[2] and though we have no evidence that he developed the views attributed to him before he reached the Continent, the heresy evidently had the effect of bringing Britain into closer contact with continental ecclesiastical matters than anything had done before.

It is clear from what we are told by Prosper of Aquitaine, one of the leading opponents of Pelagius, and also our chief informant, that Pope Celestine (*d*. 432) looked upon the Pelagian heresy as a grave menace to the unity of the Church in the West, and also that he regarded Britain as the stronghold of those holding the so-called Pelagian views. Prosper states that Celestine commanded that those holding these views were to be banished from all Italy, and adds that:

He was at no less pains to free Britain from the same plague; for certain men who were 'enemies of Grace' [the common phrase used by Prosper and others to denote the Pelagians] had taken possession of the land of their birth and were driven out (*exclusi*) from that ocean retreat by Celestine.[3]

[1] For a summary of the teaching of Pelagius, see Georges de Plinval, *Pélage, ses écrits, sa vie, et sa réforme* (Lausanne, 1943), pp. 150 ff.

[2] See de Plinval, op. cit., pp. 57 ff.

[3] *Contra Collatorem*, xxi (Migne, *P.L.* 51, col. 271).

Celestine is the first bishop of Rome who is known to have taken an active interest in our islands, but he evidently regarded this 'ocean retreat' as a serious danger to the Church as a whole; for Prosper's Chronicle, written in southern Gaul at this time, informs us s.a. 429 that a certain man holding Pelagian views, Agricola by name, son of a Pelagian bishop Severianus, was 'corrupting the churches of Britain by the secret inculcation (*insinuatio*) of his dogma', but that, at the suggestion of the deacon Palladius, Celestine sent Germanus, bishop of Auxerre, as his own representative, and that Germanus overthrew the heretics and guided the Britons to the Catholic faith.[1] We do not know who Palladius was. The name is a common one; but the office of deacon was a highly important one at this time,[2] and he may well have been identical with the Palladius who, so Prosper again tells us two years later in the same Chronicle, was ordained by Celestine and sent as first bishop to the Irish 'believing in Christ' (*credentes in Christo*).

Prosper's testimony is beyond question. He was a highly educated man, a zealous supporter of St. Augustine, with whom he corresponded personally, and a life-long opponent of Pelagianism. His early literary life was spent in the neighbourhood of Marseilles, and from there, shortly after Germanus's mission to Britain, he moved to Rome and became a *notarius* in the papal chancellery. His opportunities for acquiring precise information on matters regarding the Pelagians, and by

[1] *Epitoma Chronicon*, s.a. 429.

[2] It was the third in the Orders of the Church, following the bishop and presbyter. For the prestige of the deacon at this time, and history of the office and its nature and scope, see Cabrol, s.v., *Dictionnaire d'archéologie chrétienne et de liturgie* (Paris, 1901; in progress).

implication on Britain, are therefore especially fortunate; but our islands would have been wholly outside the orbit of his interests had it not been for their association with this particular heresy. His interest in Britain is, in fact, purely incidental.

Who then are the Irish *credentes in Christo* to whom Palladius was sent as their first bishop? Prosper's notice clearly implies that there were Christian communities in Ireland before 431 sufficiently organized to justify Rome in sending a bishop to minister to their needs.[1] It has sometimes been suggested that these communities were already affected by Pelagianism. This would certainly help to account for Celestine's mission and for Prosper's interest in it; but if this were the case Prosper would almost certainly have mentioned it. This, however, is a question which need not concern us here. For us the importance of Prosper's notice lies in its unequivocal implication that already in the early fifth century there were Christian communities in Ireland, and that Celestine was aware of them and concerned to include them within the Roman obedience. This, then, is the position in our islands up to the time when our direct continental evidence comes to an end, and our Irish evidence for St. Patrick begins. Clearly there were already Christians in Ireland before St. Patrick's mission.

It is known that about this time writing was introduced into Ireland, and though it was not first

[1] In an interesting article Professor E. A. Thompson has shown that the Roman authorities took little active part in missionary enterprise as such beyond the borders of the Empire. Their care and attention were directed to communities already Christian, and sufficiently organized to make it advisable to send a bishop ('Christianity and the Northern Barbarians', *Nottingham Medieval Studies*, i (1957), pp. 3 ff.).

introduced by Patrick himself, our first two considerable documents are believed to be from his hand. The date of St. Patrick's arrival in Ireland as a missionary from somewhere in western Britain, probably Strathclyde or Galloway or the Solway area, is disputed, but the *Annals of Ulster* enter his advent in 432, immediately after their opening entry (431) recording the mission of Palladius, who had been 'ordained by the bishop of Rome, Celestine, as first bishop of the Scots (Irish)'. This annal of the arrival of Palladius is obviously derived from Prosper. But the coincidence of the dates of the arrival of Palladius sent by Celestine, and of the arrival of Patrick himself, and of the death of Celestine in the same year (432), is surely significant. This is exactly the time when Pelagianism was powerful in Britain. It is exactly the time when Celestine was most anxious to enfold our Western Isles in the orthodoxy and organization of the Catholic Church. He had sent St. Germanus three years earlier. There is absolutely no inherent improbability in the claim of the Irish annals that St. Patrick went to Ireland, or that Palladius also went, perhaps at the same time.

The fact that we know nothing further which is reliable and of any independent value about Palladius in Ireland or Britain is immaterial. The fact that the *Annals of Ulster* record the death of Patrick at varying dates, e.g. 457 for 8 ('*Sen Patrick*'),[1] 461 for 2 ('Here some record the death of Patrick'),[2] and again much later 491, also 492 for 3, is probably due to the composite nature of the annals. Such double entries are common,

[1] 'Quies Senis Patricii ut alii libri dicunt.'
[2] 'Hoc alii quietem Patricii dicunt.' These two dates probably represent a single original and are accepted by J. Bury and E. McNeill.

and often due to the scribe's having used more than one source; and though we are here dealing with a difference of a whole generation, this is not sufficient ground for identifying the Patrick of the first obit with Palladius, or for postulating two Patricks.[1] Which of the three dates, 458, 462, or 493 has the greatest claim is a difficult question into which we cannot enter here; and moreover this serious discrepancy of a whole generation is one which runs through all our records of fifth-century Irish history.[2] Even if we were to accept the later date for Patrick's death his mission would still fall within the fifth century, and his work would still be subject to the same Roman outlook. But the most remarkable fact is that no contemporary writer anywhere mentions St. Patrick. Moreover, neither Gildas nor Bede mentions him. Plummer tried to cut the Gordian knot by denying his very existence.[3]

Every question connected with St. Patrick bristles with difficulties. Our earliest evidence for the mission of St. Patrick to Ireland, and for the Church which he is claimed to have founded there, is recorded in his own writings, notably the *Confession* and the *Letter to the Soldiers of Coroticus*, especially the *Confession*. These are, in fact, the earliest considerable documents which we possess from Ireland. Both are very short, especially the *Letter*; but both are of paramount importance, especially the *Confession*. The contents of the *Confession* claim that St. Patrick came to Ireland in response to an invitation from the friends in Ireland among whom he had spent

[1] So T. F. O'Rahilly, *The Two Patricks* (Dublin, 1942).

[2] On this matter see James Carney, *Studies in Irish Literature and History* (Dublin, 1955), ch. ix, 'Patrick and the Kings'. Cf. also H. M. Chadwick, *Early Scotland* (Cambridge, 1949), pp. 133 ff.

[3] *Baedae Historia Ecclesiastica*, i. 25.

his boyhood as a slave, and that on this second visit
he converted the Irish to Christianity and founded a
Church. Moreover the narratives of his first two biographers, Muirchu and Tirechán, who wrote towards
the close of the seventh century, and who both seem to
have had some traditions of at least a generation earlier
before them,[1] are completely consistent with this picture.
We have very few early records. We have no early
vitae as survivals, no *acta*, and very few early traditions
of the saint's companions or disciples: but such as sur-
vive, and others incorporated into later compositions,
and all the knowledge which we glean from other sources,
lead us to believe that the Church which he claims
to have formed was completely Roman in character
and tradition. Prosper has already told us that Palladius
had been sent in 431 in the same tradition. Whatever
the relationship between Palladius and Patrick, if any
indeed existed, whatever the precise date we like to
adopt for the death of Patrick, the Church which Patrick is believed to have founded in Ireland is completely
Roman in character and episcopal in government. It
falls within the fifth century.

Patrick's writings are our earliest evidence for Christianity in our islands from the time that continental evidence ceases.

For our present purpose there is no need to enter into
the question of their genuineness. Like everything else
connected with St. Patrick they present many difficulties,

[1] See, for example, Newport J. D. White, *St. Patrick, His Writings
and Life* (London, 1920), pp. 24, 68 f.; and more recently the works of
Ludwig Bieler, which include a critical text, translation, and commentary on St. Patrick's writings (2 vols., Dublin, 1952); cf. also Bieler,
Life and Legend of St. Patrick (Dublin, 1949), p. 24 f.

especially chapter iv of the *Confession*, to which I shall refer again later. In general they are accepted by most scholars as substantially his own work. It is claimed that their contents point clearly to a date about the middle of the fifth century.[1] We may refer especially to the nature of his Latin, free from Hisperic characteristics; to the text of the Scriptures which he uses so very frequently, and which favours the middle of the fifth century, a mixed text, partly Old Latin, partly Vulgate.[2] In fact both the style and Latinity are exactly what we should expect from a provincial Roman in direct contact with continental tradition; and the allusions to the heathenism of the Franks and perhaps to Mithraism (a popular cult throughout the Roman Empire at this time) amply bear out Prosper's insistence on the close contact between Britain and the Continent at this period. The reference to Coroticus seems to give us a genuine contact with the Ceredig Gwledig of the well-attested Strathclyde genealogy of this time. Moreover, in these writings Britain is still a part of the Roman Empire, and the statement that Patrick's father was a deacon and his grandfather a presbyter is in accordance with the provincial Roman married clergy at this time. He evidently regards himself as a Roman citizen, and his fellow countrymen also. The writings contain nothing which suggests a later forgery.

Yet the whole body of Patrician literature lands us in

[1] See N. J. D. White, op. cit. pp. 1 ff.

[2] This is perhaps an unsafe test, however, in an outlying province like Ireland, since we know that in Spain the use of the Old Latin Bible went on side by side with the Vulgate till well into the Middle Ages throughout the Peninsula. See Bishko, 'The Spanish Consensoria', *American Journal of Philology*, lxix (1948), p. 384.

a paradox. Little is known of his immediate successors.[3]
No great ecclesiastical establishment in Ireland in the
Age of the Saints claims its foundation from any of his
disciples. When it comes before us in the sixth century
the Irish Church is presented to us as a wholly monastic
one, and St. Patrick and his writings are out of the picture. We do not hear in any credible source of Palladius
or his mission. Church organization, church finances,
church lands are governed, not by bishops, but by
abbots. We do not know the nature of the Church
previous to the mission of Palladius, but between the
Church of the Patrician documents of the fifth century
and the Church of the sixth century the cleavage appears
to be complete. The sparsity and very diverse nature of
our documents makes this paradox particularly difficult
to account for.

To attempt to solve our problem by intensive scrutiny
of the texts alone, or by the light of later traditions, is
a hopeless quest. The differences in the organization of
the Church conceived by the Patrician writings and that
of the monastic church of the sixth century is a fundamental one, even though we must insist that this difference is one of emphasis and organization, never of
belief or of spiritual prerogative. I find it impossible
to accept the explanation commonly offered that the
differences can be accounted for by the difficulty of
continental contacts owing to the Saxon pirates on the
continental sea-routes. We have seen that communication was easy enough to enable the Pelagians in

---

[3] We have the *Hymn of St. Sechnall* (St. Secundinus) whose obit is
placed in the annals in 447, and which Bury regarded as contemporary,
but this does not seem likely. See J. Kenney, *Sources for the Early History of
Ireland* (New York, 1929), pp. 258 ff.

Britain to be a source of grave concern to Pope Celestine, who kept a close surveillance on them. There can be little doubt that the difference between the Patrician Church and the so-called Celtic Church is a more serious one, and of a different origin, as I hope to make clear in my next lecture.

At the beginning of the present lecture we saw something of the Classical spirit and tradition still lingering in Gaul, and also of the organization of the Christian Church in Gaul as a natural development of the church organization within the framework of the Roman civil system; of the local choice of bishops; of the bishops' sees being in the cities; of the local and highly organized functions of the bishop and the deacon of the parish church for their flocks. We also noted the disturbing element of monasticism entering from the East, and the background of the eastern ascetics which had inspired it. Let us look for a moment at St. Patrick's writings, which never mention monasticism,[1] and are free from mysticism, and which we have seen to be wholly Roman in character. Let us see to what elements in the Church of Gaul in the fifth century they offer the closest correspondence.

How far do Patrick's own writings reflect the contemporary atmosphere of the Church on the Continent to which they fundamentally belong? To me they do not suggest the isolation of Britain in the fifth century, or that it was in consequence of her isolation that the Celtic Church developed on lines differing widely from the Roman Church of the Continent. Patrick's Latin, despite its poor quality, is the ordinary Latin of the Schools, such as we should expect from a provincial Roman of a remote western province. It is poor and

[1] The references in Patrick's *Confession* (41, 42) are not to organized monasticism but to preceding practices and institutions in Early Christian communities. See *Studia Anselmiana*, no. 46.

crabbed in quality; but he was a Celtic speaker, not only using a foreign tongue, but writing in it; and to one of his provincial education the act of writing was doubtless itself no such handy process as it is to us. Moreover Patrick was not out of touch with *Romania*, or wholly ignorant of her culture, poor though his own version of it is. The most cursory glance at the literary form of his compositions reveals allusions and conventions of style which are current in the Gaulish compositions of the period. Even in reproving Coroticus through an open letter to his soldiers he is adopting the literary form most in favour among the literati of Gaul in his day,[1] whose correspondence was largely written with an eye to publication.

It is significant that both the form and the title of the *Confession* are of foreign origin. The title at once recalls St. Augustine's *Confessions*; but the word does not indicate a 'confession' in the modern sense. It means a *depositio*, a 'deposition', and is related to the 'Confessors' of the time of the persecutions, i.e. those who made their *depositio*, who 'subscribed' to the Faith.[2] Botte has argued cogently[3] that while during the persecutions the word referred to those who made their *depositio* in defence of the faith against paganism, the word extended

[1] The anonymous letters first published by Caspari, and believed to date from this period and to have been written, in part at least, by Britons, would seem to suggest that in Britain also the form may have been in vogue. For an easily accessible version in English translation of this most interesting collection the reader may be referred to R. S. T. Haslehurst, *The Works of Fastidius* (London, 1927).

[2] For an interesting discussion of the word see J. E. L. Oulton, *The Credal Statements of St. Patrick* (London, 1940), p. 8. Oulton points out that chs. 3, 4, and 5 are connected verbally by the recurrence of the word 'confess' (*confiteri*).

[3] 'Confessor', *Archivum Latinitatis Medii Aevi*, xvi (1942), pp. 137 ff.

in the fourth and fifth centuries to denote those who defended it against heresy, who 'subscribed' to the Faith—in the fourth century against Arianism, in the fifth against Pelagianism. St. Augustine, he argues, used the word in this latter sense. Patrick was no theologian, but his 'confession', probably in the same literary and semantic tradition as St. Augustine's, might be described as an *apologia pro vita sua*, a spiritual autobiography, composed to justify his divine calling.

Moreover the form of the opening of St. Patrick's *Confession*, beginning with a brief mention of his family and early life, his youthful 'sin', his failure to apply himself duly to his studies—all this echoes his greater continental predecessor,[1] and leads one to wonder if, in fact, his sin was ever really committed, and was not just a literary commonplace. The habit of referring to oneself as *peccator* was a part of the current religious jargon of the day, as is shown by the signatures of all the letters signed jointly by St. Paulinus of Nola and his wife Therasia—'Paulinus et Therasia, *peccatores*'.

Further, St. Patrick's use of this current religious diction is to be seen also in the opening formula of self-abasement in his *Letter to Coroticus's soldiers*: 'Patrick the sinner, unlearned truly'. This literary cliché professing ignorance and rusticity is met again on the lips of Gallus, the *scholasticus* from St. Martin's monastery at Tours, who in the *Dialogues* of Sulpicius Severus professes himself as 'blushing' and hesitating to speak before cultured Aquitanians; but in fact these expressions are the mark of polish and literary good breeding, an oratorical cliché, as Posthumianus does not fail to remark: 'As you are an orator (*scholasticus*) you carefully, after the fashion of

[1] Cf. especially St. Augustine, *Confessions*, I. viii, II, III.

C

orators, begin by begging us to excuse your unskilful-ness because you really excel in eloquence.'

This modesty was no less a convention than the spiritual self-abasement of the medieval religious. It was a part of the literary polish of the panegyrists, such as Pacatus. Patrick shows himself well aware of the exis-tence of the class of men known as *rhetorici*, to whom he refers more than once. In general it may be said that he partook of the literary life of Gaul as this was reflected in provincial Britain in his day, much as the funerary lapidary inscriptions derive their style and epigraphi-cal features from the corresponding inscriptions on the Continent.

His use of current phrases in a purely conventional sense has been interpreted literally, and this has given rise to error. In the *Confession* he says, 'This is my con-fession before I die', and this is generally understood to indicate that the work was composed late in life; but in view of the technical meaning of *confessio*, may we not suspect rather an echo of the formula of a *confessor*, a traditional expression from the days of martyrdom, rather than a declaration of old age? Again, his state-ment that during his mission the Gospel has been carried 'to the limit beyond which no man dwells' is commonly understood to refer to the west of Ireland; but the phrase is only a slight variant of the static for-mula for the British Isles throughout our period as used by all continental writers, and is to be found in the writings of St. Paula, of the Bordeaux Pilgrim, of Ruti-lius Namatianus, and many others. We may compare St. Patrick's own words later in the same work in reference to his missionary efforts 'in the ends of the earth' (*in ultimis terrae*).

Patrick's fondness for dreams as a literary motif links him with fourth- and fifth-century continental writers, among whom the theme was a special favourite. We think first of St. Jerome's famous dream in which he saw himself castigated before the throne of God for his incurable love of Cicero. Ausonius was subject to nightmares[1] hardly less terrifying. Then there is St. Martin,[2] and St. Augustine himself.[3] In the small compass of his writings Patrick reports three dreams. In one of them—'a vision of the night'—a man whom he calls Victor—or as we should say, a postman—'coming as it were from Ireland with countless letters, bearing on them the name and address of the senders', hands one of his pile to Patrick which invites him to revisit his old friends. Is it just an accident that the postman's name is Victor, identical with that of the letter-carrier who bore letters annually from St. Paulinus of Nola to his friend Sulpicius Severus of Aquitaine, and that these included invitations to visit him in his home in Italy? It is only by later writers that St. Patrick's Victor is transformed into an angel.

The contents of chapter iv of the *Confession* offer perhaps the most important evidence of all for the dependence of St. Patrick's writings on contemporary continental literature, in this case on theological, especially credal, literature. Professor Oulton has shown[4] that this chapter cannot claim to be the original work of the

[1] In his poem *Ephemeris* he enumerates all the principal kinds of dreams and nightmares to which he is habitually subject.
[2] Sulpicius Severus, *Vita*, iii, v. I omit dreams of the 'incubation' type, deliberately induced, related of St Martin (*Vita*, xi).
[3] *Confessions*, x. xxx; ibid. iii. xi; *City of God*, xiv. xix.
[4] Oulton, *The Credal Statements of St. Patrick* (London, 1940), Preface and *passim*.

writer of the *Confessions* in exactly the same sense that
the rest of the work is original.[1] Its general structure, its
creed-like contents, its phraseology indicate that the
author was acquainted with the *Commentary on the Apo-
calypse* by Victorinus of Pettau[2] in the recension of that
work made by St. Jerome *c.* A.D. 406.[3] Further, apart
from phrases borrowed from this work, the theological expressions in this chapter can almost all be paral-
leled in Gallican writers[4] and documents[5] of the fourth
and fifth centuries. The whole chapter is expressed in
a better style than the rest of the *Confession;* and this
Oulton attributes to the fact that the author is here
'adopting or echoing phrases which he has found to
hand'. Oulton concludes with the interesting reflection
that the 'Gallican tradition within which Patrick stands
is consistent with other facts revealed by his credal
statements'; and that 'analysis of the text of chapter 4
of the *Confession* brings its author into touch with Gaul,
Spain, Milan, and finally Pannonia'. For further echoes
of contemporary and slightly earlier theological expressions I must refer the reader to Oulton's study, which
is a valuable testimony to the familiarity of the writer
of the Patrician documents with contemporary continental writings. It may be added that Père Grosjean,
Bollandiste, has recently claimed that St. Patrick had also
had access to a letter of St. Jerome to Pope Damasus.[6]

---

[1] Ibid., p. 11.   [2] Martyred in the Diocletian persecution, *c.* A.D. 304.
[3] See on this point Oulton, p. 34.
[4] Ibid., pp. 12, 15 ('Emphasis on the Trinity is a marked feature of
Gallican creeds and writers'), 31.
[5] For some interesting explicit references see Oulton, op. cit., p. 34;
cf. also pp. 29 f.
[6] See *St. Patrick*, edited by the Revd. F. J. Ryan S. J. (Dublin, 1958),
p. 65.

From all this it is clear that the author of the Patrician documents, although a provincial, was no isolated rustic, but was a partaker in the cultured thought of the western Europe of his own day. In strong contrast to the saint portrayed in the writings of Muirchu and Tirechán in the late seventh century, and still more to that in the *Tripartite Life* in the ninth, the saint of these writings comes before us as the product of the Classical tradition and the Classical education of a Roman province of the fifth century—'on the edge of the habitable globe', but still one with a claim to be a citizen of the Empire. The son of a deacon (a high official of the Church), the grandson of a presbyter, he had a background not essentially different from that of Gaulish bishops of the period. Yet his writings speak throughout of difficulties and opposition, not from the heathen, but from his own colleagues, where he felt he had reason to look for sympathy and support for his work. He is concerned throughout to justify his episcopal office, and to claim a divine calling for his mission.

It is generally recognized that our Patrician documents, and the writings of the saint's immediate successors, imply the existence of an episcopal Church in Ireland in the fifth century comparable with the contemporary episcopal organization of the Church in Gaul, and I have tried to show that the *Letter* and the *Confession* reflect the literary conventions of Gaul at the same period. Let us once more turn to Gaul, therefore, to look for the reason of St. Patrick's mission, and of the rapid growth of the monastic Church in the following century. We have seen that the Gaulish Church had developed on the lines of the Roman civil service. The Gaulish Church was essentially an urban Church, based on ancient legal and administrative precedent. The bishop had his see, his *sedes*, in the cities, which were the administrative centres of the province. This was in all probability the original form of church organization in the Roman province of Britain also, with which Patrick would be familiar, at least to some extent.

Into this system, deeply rooted in Gaul and in the western Mediterranean areas, a new and disturbing influence penetrated from the eastern Mediterranean in the fourth century, and rapidly spread as a living force throughout the whole area. This was no less than the monastic eremitical movement to which I referred at the beginning of my lecture and to which I must now return. It was essentially democratic, and it brought with it new ideals of spiritual specialization and withdrawal. Ausonius saw it as the end of the Classical world, as indeed it was. To his pupil, the great Aquitanian noble St. Paulinus of Nola, it came as a religious revelation of dazzling brilliance. This monastic organization was independent of the old established ecclesiastical system. The principles by which it was governed were not unnaturally regarded by the established Church as disruptive of both the social and the ecclesiastical system which had hitherto governed church preferment, especially in the matter of episcopal elections. In accordance with the monastic ideal of poverty and the equality of man in the eyes of God, the leading men of the new system were often men of no prestige, often foreigners, making no claim to social status, but rather what we should now call displaced persons. Even their name and the country of their origin were sometimes unknown,[1] in accordance with the new ideal of giving up

[1] We are told by Eugippius in his *Vita* of St. Severinus (d. 482), the

their home and country and becoming a *peregrinus* to God. In consequence a spirit of hostility towards these new-comers rapidly grew up in Gaulish episcopal circles. The contemporary writings of Sulpicius Severus are largely directed to vindicating his hero, St. Martin of Tours, the pioneer of the monastic movement in Gaul, against the hostility of the bishops; and we gather from the correspondence of Sulpicius with his lifelong friend, St. Paulinus of Nola, that he himself, living an ascetic life in Aquitaine, was also suffering from hostility from the Gaulish bishops. This hostility was widely known in Italy and the East. In 392 St. Ambrose makes these episcopal quarrels his excuse for not going to Gaul.[1] In 406 Jerome, in his treatise against Vigilantius, refers, with bitter abuse, to the opposition to asceticism in Gaul.[2]

In the early years of the fifth century this growing hostility between the episcopal and the monastic elements became articulate, and centred largely in the election of bishops. Celestine, the bishop of Rome, who had died shortly after sending Palladius as bishop to Ireland, had expressed himself forcibly on the subject of the new movement in his famous letter *Cuperemus quidem* (25 July 428) addressed to the bishops of Vienne and Narbonne. In this letter he had condemned the practice of appointing 'wanderers and strangers' (*peregrini et extranei*) over the heads of the local clergy, who were known to their flocks and had a right to look for preferment in the district where they had spent their

apostle in Pannonia and Noricum on the Danube, that the saint never to the end of his life revealed his name or the place of his origin.
[1] 'Gallorum episcoporum, propter quorum frequentes dissensiones crebro me excusaveram' (*De Obitu Valentiniani Consolatio*).
[2] *Contra Vigilantium.*

lives: 'Let no one', he urges, 'in any way steal into the
sphere of someone else, or dare to appropriate the reward which is another man's right', and he makes no
secret of his dislike of monastic bishops, for elsewhere in
the same letter he writes pointedly enough:

It is not surprising that they who have not grown up in
the Church act contrary to the Church's usages, and that,
coming from other customs, they have brought their traditional ways with them into our Church. Clad in a cloak, and
with a girdle round the loins, they consider that they will
be fulfilling the letter rather than the spirit of the Scriptures.
. . . Such a practice may perhaps be followed as a matter of
course rather than reason by those who dwell in remote
places and pass their lives far from their fellow men. But
why should they dress in this way in the Churches of God,
changing the usage of so many years, of such great prelates,
for another habit?[1]

Turning again to St. Patrick and the difficulties and
obstruction of which he complains, the nature of the
early Patrician Church and the rapid growth of the
monastic organization which overshadows it in our traditions of the centuries immediately following, I think
these can perhaps be explained most readily against
this background of controversy in Gaul. The background of the Patrick of these documents is that of an
ecclesiastical landed family in Roman Britain. It is comparable to that of the territorial bishops and clergy in
urban Gaul. His care to record his immediate forebears
and the place of his home is in strong contrast to Celestine's *peregrini* and *extranei*. Yet in spite of Celestine's
opposition monastic bishops continued to be appointed
in Gaul, and monasticism spread.

[1] *Ep.* 4, Mansi III, p. 264; Migne, *P.L.* l, col. 430.

In Ireland the rapidity with which it seems to have spread and gained complete predominance must have been largely due to the fact that there had never been a Roman occupation. There were no cities. The economy was wholly pastoral and in no way remotely resembled the Roman urban or civil system. In Ireland and western Scotland the new monasticism had only to adjust itself to a hereditary system of royal landowners, the local kings. In Europe, as Kenney has observed,[1] the normal monastery was more or less withdrawn from the world, and the normal parish church was not a monastery. In Ireland, where there were no cities, the monastery served as the natural gathering point for the scattered rural population, and the monastic system of the Celtic Church was essentially adapted to a pastoral people, the only recognized unit being the *túath*, with its centre in the royal *rath*. But a Church developing exclusively, or almost exclusively, on these lines was what Celestine deprecated.

We have seen that during Celestine's lifetime at least, Britain was by no means isolated from continental contacts, and so the controversy between the territorial and the monastic bishops in Gaul can hardly have been without repercussions in our islands. Patrick never makes any categorical claim to have visited Gaul; but he expresses a longing to visit his 'friends' there (not to 'revisit') and in view of his Roman outlook and education there could have been no question on which side in the controversy his sympathies would have lain. There is no hint of either mysticism or monasticism in his works, or even that he was aware of such things, though the *Cuperemus quidem* was exactly contemporary with the dates

[1] *Sources for the Early History of Ireland* (New York, 1929), p. 473, n. 318.

assigned to the missions of both Palladius and Patrick. He belonged to the 'old school'. His sojourn in Gaul is an unfounded assumption.

Unfortunately the testimony of Prosper fails us for Britain, for the dispute lay outside his interests, and we have almost no records for the British Church to help us. But both the mission claimed for St. Patrick in the documents under his name, and also the opposition which he encountered, could be explained without difficulty if we could suppose that he came as a member of the conservative episcopal party—if he was known to represent a party in the Church pledged to counteract the growing power and prestige of monasticism, and of monastic preferment to episcopal sees. His mission and that of Palladius both follow immediately on the period of Celestine's active interest in Britain—his strenuous efforts against the Pelagians; his missions; his sending St. Germanus—another territorial bishop of the 'old school'—and also Palladius. Patrick's difficulties in establishing at this early date a strong episcopal Church in Ireland would be readily accounted for if this form of church government was in the fifth century felt to be old-fashioned, and somewhat out-moded, and was losing prestige before the spread of monasticism and asceticism.

These features in the continental background may help to account for the form of Patrick's mission—as distinct from his 'call'—and also for his initial difficulties, and possibly for some hard-won success. It is tempting to regard it as a part of an attempt of the episcopal party, of the 'old school', inspired—perhaps only indirectly—and supported initially by Celestine, and further by the bishops of Gaul, perhaps also by some in Britain, to discourage the growing power of monasticism

in the Western Church. The mission of Palladius to
Ireland, vouched for by Prosper, may have been a part
of the same effort. This would seem especially probable
if he were identical with the deacon Palladius; while the
mission of St. Germanus to Britain in 429 and the part
played by the deacon Palladius in the arrangement link
Celestine closely with a struggle to keep the Western Isles
within the Roman obedience on traditional lines. The
forces against which the Patrician party was contend-
ing were strong. They were nothing less than the mysticism and asceticism now pervading western thought,
and introducing from the East a new way of life in
the Church, and something of a new cross-section of
society; and though the growth of monasticism did
not modify, or seek to modify, the order of the church
services, or supplant the hierarchy of the Church itself
in the Celtic countries, the monastic system attained
to such dimensions and power that it has come to be
identified with the Celtic Church itself. It will be our concern in the next lecture to try to understand this early
monasticism which infused a new enthusiasm and a more
intense devotion into the Western Church in the sixth
century, and gave it new life in the Age of the Saints.

In the meantime it will be of interest to turn to the
Eastern source of the ascetic and monastic influence
which was penetrating the Western world at the close
of the Classical period—an influence so strong and so
all-pervading that it may be said to have transformed
society. It is important that we should have a glimpse
at first hand, however brief, of the Eastern ascetics and
their ideals and discipline, if we are to understand the
nature of their influence in the West. On their mortified

life and austerities, their devotion to the highest spiritual ideals, I need not dwell. A millennium and a half has recognized and beatified this form of their sanctity. I should like to emphasize here another side of the influence of the Eastern Churches through their ascetic communities which has not been so generally appreciated in the West, namely the stimulus which they gave to the intellectual life, to the spread of reading and of book production, and to the growth of civilization through international exchange of knowledge.

I began by claiming that the Age of the Saints was fundamentally an intellectual one and that it is through the wide and swift growth of the practice of writing at this period, and the consequent dissemination of books, that it has left its mark on the history of civilization. Its paramount importance was recognized at the outset by the Emperor Constantine, who, among his other contributions to the benefit of the Church, also paid for the copying of the Scriptures.[1] He realized that writing was a prime necessity of the new religion. In fact the copying of books was a great industry in the Greek monasteries. To Evagrius, a good calligraphist, it seems to have been the chief source of income.[2] Cassian tells of a monk who was ignorant of Greek, so was set to copy a Latin text 'out of charity', though none of the brethren could read Latin.[3] Quite incidentally we hear of a certain Marcus in Scete[4] who was a copyist of ancient manuscripts.

---

[1] See S. L. Greenslade, *Church and State from Constantine to Theodosius* (London, 1954), p. 21.

[2] *The Lausiac History of Palladius*, xxxviii. 10, translated by W. K. Lowther Clarke, (London, 1918).   [3] *Institutes*, v. xxxix.

[4] *Apophthegmata*, xiv, 5. See Owen Chadwick, *Western Asceticism* (London, 1958), p. 150. For the complete text of the *Apophthegmata*, see Migne, *P. L.*, 73, cols. 851 ff.

It may safely be claimed that the special form of sanctity practised by the saints of the Celtic Church—poverty, asceticism, solitude, contemplation—could never have become a widespread movement without the communion and the stimulus which they derived from the early Church through the written word. One has only to think of the church councils, Eastern and Western, the lively part which the early Fathers took in the matters under discussion; the writings of the Fathers for the enlightenment and guidance of the faithful and of the purity of the Faith. And looking farther east, our records are unanimous in their testimony of the lively part, often a leading part, which the founders of the desert monasteries and the most extreme ascetics took in the keenly disputed problems of their day, drawing their original inspiration from the intellectual life which the Scriptures had originally stimulated and continued to stimulate and inform. The monks of the desert carried on an active correspondence. St. Jerome's letters are the best-known example, but the writings of Cassian make it clear that the monks of Egypt also carried on a lively correspondence with the outside world. The last place from which one would look for a heavy mail bag is the top of a pillar. Yet in the fifth century Daniel the pillar saint of the Bosphoros was in constant written correspondence with the Emperor and the Patriarch at Constantinople, and took a lively part in diplomatic exchanges. Round about 500 St. Sabas, perhaps the most important monastic leader in Palestine in his day, played an important diplomatic role under both Anastasius and Justinian. But it is especially in the actual writing and possession of books that the contribution of the Eastern ascetics to the spread of civilization is most impressive. Ideals of austerity are subject to fluctuation, but whatever the form of ascetic discipline, the message of the ideals which prompted the discipline is always a living message when it is written and circulated in books. And this the Eastern ascetics well knew.

This intellectual basis of the *sanctus* is easier to demonstrate in the East than in the West, for the Eastern Church had always been more intellectual than the Western. Theodoret (d. towards 460) in his *Ecclesiastical History* shows knowledge of the writings of Homer, Thucydides, Plato, Euripides, and other Classical writers, though he spent his life as bishop of a small city in the wild society between Antioch and the Euphrates.[1] We shall find fragments of the Greek Classics in the monastery of St. Epiphanius of Thebes in Upper Egypt. Eastern ascetic communities are far more numerous and widely distributed and fully documented than those of the West. It is in the East, therefore, that we can trace most readily the importance of writing in all phases of monastic life, including the ascetic communities, not only the coenobitic but also the hermits.

The records of the Egyptian and Eastern monasteries and ascetic communities are full of interesting information about the practice of writing and the conditions of book production and the attitude of the religious to books. Monastic copyists commonly worked in their cells;[2] but in the monastery of John Kamé we read of Bessus the Superior copying books during fourteen

[1] Bloomfield and Jackson, *Theodoret* (Nicene and Post-Nicene Fathers III, New York, 1892), p. 2.

[2] *Apophthegmata*, xiv, 5 (Marcus); and cf. H. G. Evelyn White, *The Monasteries of the Wadi'n Natrun, Part I. New Coptic Texts from the Monastery of St. Macarius* (New York, 1926), p. xlv.

nights, apparently on end, along with several other brethren. And we come once more on the little personal marginalia with which we are familiar from Irish manuscripts. In one manuscript from the Monastery of the Syrians in Scete in Lower Egypt an angry copyist excuses his bad writing on the grounds of badly pre-pared vellum and adds: 'Lord, help me to fight against these accursed flies,' and again: 'May God smite these flies which war with me these days.'[1]

The *Apophthegmata*,[2] or 'Traditional Sayings' of the Desert Fathers, constantly report the rebukes of the elders to monks against devotion to books privately owned by the monks, which they regard as militating against devotion to charity, in their eyes far preferable to learning. Here, however, we have to be on our guard. It is to be suspected that this reported censure of books is biased by the jealousy felt by the Copts towards the more highly educated Greeks; and this has given rise to a false notion in the west that asceticism and igno-rance go together. In fact the reverse is the case. Evagrius almost seems to rank knowledge higher than love; and the Pachomian written Rule insists that all members of the community must learn to read. And here we may recall the remarkable series of anonymous fifth-century Latin letters, believed to be probably written by a Bri-ton, to which I have already referred above, in one of which the importance of knowledge is insisted on above all other Christian virtues: 'I assert', says the writer, 'that there is no real ignorance when a man knows where his ignorance lies', and proceeds to

[1] Evelyn White, loc. cit.
[2] For selected translations, with introduction and notes, see O. Chadwick, *Western Asceticism*.

demonstrate that God requires us to make active efforts to acquire the knowledge necessary to carry out His commands. 'It is possible to know His wish, and either fulfil it or not, but it is impossible to fulfil it if you do not know it.'[1]

Books seem to have been often privately owned. They were apparently among the possessions of Theodore of Pherme seized by robbers in the fourth century[2] and we also hear of three of his books said to have been especially helpful, which he was in the habit of lending to the other brethren.[3] Paphnutius of Scete was falsely charged with the theft of a volume;[4] and the Tall Brothers in the Mountain of Nitria possessed a collection of 'excellent canonical books'.[5] Evagrius refers to a monk who had no possessions except the Gospel.[6] We read of others who wrote to furnish reading matter for themselves and others.[7] These private book collections were kept in the owners' cells in cupboards ($\theta \nu \rho \acute{\iota} \delta \epsilon s$) or 'aumbreys', niches in the walls of their cells or possibly the window recesses. The abba Serapion reproved one brother because he saw this recess full of books; and to another who had made for himself a copy of the Old and New Testaments he offered reproaches for filling up his niches with papers, while Amoi declared to his disciples that he had seen men fleeing and leaving their niches littered with parchment books.[8] It

---

[1] R. S. T. Haslehurst, *The Works of Fastidius* (London, 1927), p. 21.

[2] *Apophthegmata*. Theodore of Pherme XXIX.

[3] Ibid. Cf. O. Chadwick, *Western Asceticism*, p. 78.

[4] Cassian. *Collationes*. xviii. 15.

[5] Palladius, *Dialogues, De Vita Johannis Chrysostomi, P.G.* xlvii, I. i. 24.

[6] O. Chadwick, loc. cit. He refers to Socrates, *H.E.* iv. 23, for the Greek text for Evagrius' *Practice*.

[7] *Apophthegmata*. Abraham III.

[8] *Apophthegmata*. Theodore of Pherme XXIX.

is clear that books were a prized possession and were sometimes bought, sometimes lent, and sometimes stolen, but hardly ever willingly given or sold.

By the latter part of the sixth century, however, it would seem that the monastery of the Syrians at Scete had a collection of books for common use, i.e. a library, for in a note in a manuscript from this monastery, now in the Vatican, an inscription states that:

This book along with others was bought on the 13th of July in 576 A.D. for the holy monastery of Scetis in the days of the most religious Mar Theodore, the abbot, by the gift of God and the abbot's own money. This book he bought together with others for the contemplation, reading, and spiritual advancement of all those who shall open it. But who so shall seek this book to read it . . . and shall not return it to its owners, may he inherit the halter of Judas for ever.
                                                                    Amen.[1]

In the monastery of Macarius we hear of a monk who 'had charge of the sacred writings', and of a steward who both had charge of the books and perhaps made purchases for the monastery.[2] With the lending library of Scete in the sixth century we may compare a passage (cap. 3) in the Life of St. Daniel the Pillar Saint near Constantinople in the fifth century, written by his disciple, where we are told that 'It was the custom in monasteries that many different books should be laid in front of the sanctuary, and whichever book a brother wants he takes and reads.'[3]

Still more interesting is the information furnished by

[1] *Assemanni Bibliothecae Apostolicae Vaticanae Catalogus*, iii, no. cxliii (pp. 245 ff.).   [2] Evelyn White, op. cit., xliv.
[3] E. Dawes and N. H. Baynes, *Three Byzantine Saints*, translated from the Greek (Oxford, 1948), p. 8.

Crum from the papyri and ostraca of the monastery of Epiphanius at Thebes in Upper Egypt[1] of *c.* A.D. 600 where some Greek still survived for liturgical use, and some few surviving Greek texts seem to be school exercises.[2] We find among the Greek secular works lines from the Iliad; and more than one selection of sentences from Menander,[3] a quotation from the Greek anthology; a medical book; two magical texts; a small fragment in double columns of a glossary in Greek and Coptic.[4] And we may accept the word of this very experienced scholar that 'The books read by these Thebans would seem to have been . . . of much the same character as those which furnished monastic libraries further south and north.' The most interesting of the texts from the Theban site is a list of books—a catalogue—on a limestone flake bearing the title 'The List (λόγος) of the holy books of the τόπος of Apa Elias of the Rock', and the first division contains thirty-three entries, mostly Biblical; the second twenty-four, patristic; the third twenty-two, miscellaneous.[5]

We hear relatively little of the intellectual life of Lower Egypt, and in fact the evidence of the *Apophthegmata* appears to be deliberately selected to create the impression that learning and books were inimical to higher demands, among which charity is held to have stronger claims. I have already suggested that this is to be accepted only with some reserve in view of the Coptic jealousy of the educated Greeks. When we move with Hilarion to Gaza or with Euthemius and Evagrius to

[1] Winlock and Crum, *The Monastery of Epiphanius at Thebes* (New York, 1926), pp. 220 f.
[2] Yet generally speaking Menander does not seem to have been much used as a school textbook.   [3] Winlock and Crum, op. cit.., p. 196.
[4] Ibid., pp. 206 f.   [5] Ibid., p. 197.

Palestine the importance of knowledge is held to be paramount, though they had received their ascetic training in Egypt. Many of the disciples of Euthemius had distinguished careers in the Greek Church, and his own monastery (*lavra*) had a close contact with Juvenal, the most outstanding figure in the monastic life of Jerusalem, with its stress on the Psalmody and the Liturgy, which are among the chief gifts of the Eastern to the Western Church. In the hymns of the ascetics Euthemius is placed only second to St. Antony; and his successor, St. Sabas, was a leader of the Judaean monasticism which for centuries developed the hymnody and liturgy of the Eastern Order, and preserved the continuity of its intellectual life which culminated in John of Damascus. Here, nevertheless many ascetics and 'grazers' (βοσκοί) joined him, as we shall find Suibhne Geilt the Irish fanatical saint joining St. Moling in his retreat.[1]

Our fullest knowledge about the books and intellectual life of an ascetic community comes from Beth Abhê, 'The House of the Forest', founded at the end of the sixth century on a mountain peak in Mesopotamia. It was an off-shoot of the 'great monastery' of Nisibis where the first Christian ascetics of Mesopotamia had established themselves under Mar Awgin of Clysma, near Suez, early in the fourth century. Beth Abhê was a Nestorian monastery of high ecclesiastical standing, and its monks were renowned for their learning. Its history[2] was written by the monk Thomas of Marga in the ninth century, and from many notices in his work we are able to piece

---

[1] These βοσκοί are said to have been introduced into Syria already very early in the fourth century by one Aones. See Sozomen, *H.E*, vi. 33.
[2] Translated by E. A. W. Budge, *Historia Monastica of Thomas, Bishop of Marga, A.D. 840* (London, 1893).

together the growth of a great monastic library during the sixth and seventh centuries.

The enthralling account of how this remote monastic library was built up tempts one to linger here. The first book was obtained by Shamtâ the 'tax-gatherer', the 'advocate of the Church' from Edessa, where Khosroe had sent him to obtain 'copies of the Scriptures and prayer books and lectionaries' for the new convent which he had built for his Christian queen. Among them was a large service-book, of which it would appear the Catholicos made a number of copies with his own hand.[1] Many of the books in the library can be traced by direct copying and recopying through Nisibis to Scete. Among the most interesting are those of the famous Anan-Isho, author of the classic *Paradise* and of a number of philosophical and scholarly works. It is interesting to note that all his own books and those of his brother were inherited by their nephew John who transferred them as a gift to the monastic library, as did also his *syncellus* Dindowai, and as did also another pious and learned monk who during a raid had come with all his books to Beth Abhê, and who bequeathed them before his death to its library.[2] Among the most interesting collections was that of Bäbhai, the musician and founder and organizer of the Schools, and writer of funeral orations, a metrical homily, and many hymns of praise, as well as twenty-two on Jacob, the founder of the monastery. The chief treasure of the monastery, however, was a magnificent 'Golden Gospel Book', which the Catholicos himself appropriated during a visit to the monastery early in the eighth century when the monastery was in a period of decline; but the monks

---

[1] Budge, op. cit., p. lix.   [2] Ibid. ii. 236, 282.

pursued him furiously and retrieved it with some vio-
lence.[1] The history of this library is particularly fascinating. We can trace, as it were, the personal history
of the books.

It is clear that in Beth Abhê, as in Egypt, the monks
possessed and bequeathed books as their own property,
and at Beth Abhê learning and book production flourished
on a grand scale. The books were highly prized, and
only one case of a sale of books is recorded, and that
only as a matter of dire necessity. The incident is significant. Rabban Simon and his three disciples had taken
refuge in a cave, apparently during a raid on their
monastery,[2] and after Simon's death one of his disciples,
compelled by famine, took the books which Simon had
written, and went down to the villages, to sell them and
bring back food.[3] Budge estimates that when Thomas
wrote the history of Beth Abhê early in the ninth century the library contained between 700 and 1,000 books.

This is not to claim that all the inmates of the
coenobium or the *lavra* were intellectual or even literate. It
is well known that this was not the case; and also that as
they advanced in their ascetic discipline even the most
accomplished perhaps set less store on books. The life
of the contemplative passes ultimately into realms
where it draws its inspiration from spiritual sources independent of books. It would not be true to claim an
intellectual equipment even for all the great leaders of
monasticism, far less for every one of their followers. Yet
even this slight survey makes it clear that ignorance was
not valued for its own sake, and that it is to the literate

---

[1] Ibid. ii. 282.
[2] Three successive Arab raids cleared out the library of St. Macarius
in Scete.   [3] Ibid. ii., cap. xxv, pp. 226 f.

and intellectual equipment of the Eastern ascetics that we are indebted for our knowledge of the earliest Western asceticism and community life. Without St. Athanasius's brilliant biography of St. Antony, without Cassian's *Dialogues*,[1] the life of the desert hermits would have been little known in the West in early times.

In Gaul and western Europe the ascetic way of life never exercised the power over the imagination or resulted in the widespread practice as an institution that it attained in the East. The development of city life in Gaul and its close-knit organization militated against the detachment and individualism of the solitary life. Moreover the organization of the Church and the prerogative of the bishops were powerful forces against the more extreme forms of ascetic practice. Gregory of Tours tells us of a deacon Wulfolaic, a Lombard by birth, who entertained him in his monastery at Yvi, the modern Carignan in the Ardennes, and who had formerly set up a column near Trèves and lived on its summit as a stylite; but the local bishops persuaded him to abandon it and live among his own converts; and then one day during his absence they had the column destroyed.[2]

Nevertheless in the less populous areas of Gaul a considerable measure of eremitism evidently developed during the sixth century. An interesting letter of Sidonius Apollinaris[3] includes an elegy which he had composed

---

[1] For the position of Cassian as an intermediary between Eastern and Western monasticism, see O. Chadwick, *John Cassian* (Cambridge, 1950).

[2] *Hist. Franc.* viii. 15. Cf. also Delehaye, *Les Saints stylites* (1923), pp. cxlii–clxiii.

[3] Book VII, xvii. Cf. also Gregory of Tours, *Vitae Patrum*, iii.

for the ascetic Abraham, who had escaped from prison on the Euphrates during the persecutions instituted by Yezdigerd and continued under his successor Bahram V,[1] and who had eventually settled in Clermont, where he had founded the community of St. Cierges, and where he had died in 477. Still earlier in the same century the author of an anonymous poem, the *Carmen de Providentia Divina* (v. 49 ff.) written *c.* 415 or 416, perhaps by Prosper of Aquitaine, in reference to the Barbarian Invasions, speaks of the sufferings of the solitaries 'who had no other occupation in their caves and caverns than to praise God day and night'.[2]

The passage recalls the early settlement of St. Martin at Ligugé, where the monks are said to have occupied separate cells or caves in the rocks; but the reference in our poem may very possibly be to the ascetic solitaries who during the late fifth and sixth centuries are traditionally reported to have occupied the mountains and forests of the Jura, Le Perche, and Auvergne and elsewhere. For these our chief authority is Gregory of Tours,[3] who writes as a contemporary, and who has left in his *Vitae Patrum*[4] twenty brief biographies of the early bishops, abbots, and ascetic solitaries of Gaul, as well as many further references in his *Historia Francorum*

---

[1] See Duchesne, *Early History of the Church* (English translation by C. Jenkins, 1924, reprinted 1951), iii. 388. and references.

[2] See J. R. Palanque and P. de Labriolle, *The Church in the Christian Roman Empire*, ii (London, 1952), p. 488.

[3] Sir Samuel Dill devotes a chapter to a general account of these precursors of monachism in Gaul (*Roman Society in Gaul in the Merovingian Age* (London, 1926,) pp. 355 ff.). O. M. Dalton has summarized the evidence of Gregory of Tours in i. 374 ff. of his translation of Gregory's *History of the Franks*.

[4] Translated into French by H. L. Bordier, *Les Livres des miracles ... de Georges Florent Grégorie Évêque de Tours* (Paris, 1892), pp. 132 ff.

and *De Gloria Confessorum*. For the Fathers of the Jura we also possess the Lives of SS. Romanus, Lupicinus, and Eugendius, in the *Vitae Patrum Jurensium*, an anonymous work believed to date from *c*. 550, and our most ancient and interesting document for the early monastic history of this part of Gaul.[1]

Further traditions related by Gregory and other later *vitae* also tell of other saintly hermits of this period. Gregory's sources are largely unknown.[2] He tells us that his own father had been cured by St. Martius of Auvergne,[3] who had retired from the world and hewn out a little hermitage for himself in the mountain-side, carving his bed from the solid rock.[4] Around him a community gathered who cultivated the 'desert', creating a garden and orchard. Breton legends also are full of stories of the clearance of the forest and waste and the cultivation of the soil. Gregory himself tells of a sixth-century Breton saint, named John, who had made a garden beside his cell, and who used to sit reading and writing in the shade of the trees, which had grown tall in Gregory's time.[5]

Had these stories of the Gaulish solitaries the atmosphere of romance for their original listeners which they hold for us today? One sees in all a common pattern. A recluse, seeking solitude, withdraws to a cave or cell in mountain or forest and around him a number of disciples soon gather forming first a community, each member with his own cell, till gradually the nucleus of a cenobitic institution develops into a monastery. To

[1] See Leclercq and Cabrol, *Dictionnaire* (ed. cit.), s.v. Jura.
[2] H. Delehaye, *Les Légendes hagiographiques* (Bruxelles, 1927), pp. 72 f.
[3] *Vitae Patrum*, xiv, cap. 3.   [4] Ibid., cap. 1.
[5] *De Gloria Confessorum*, cap. 23.

what extent the life of permanent total eremitism was ever widespread in Gaul may be doubted.[1] There is no evidence to suggest that it ever developed into a movement which had any direct influence in lands farther west. Yet the same influence which must have brought the anchorite impulse into Gaul in the fifth and sixth centuries, for however brief a period, must have been inspiring the countries farther west at the same time. In Brittany the foundation of the most important religious house in the interior of the country, situated in the heart of the forest of Brocéliande near Paimpont, is ascribed by tradition to St. Méen, an early settler, and a member of the royal house of Powys in Wales. Here eventually he was joined by King Judicaël of the north Breton province of Domnonia, and a great monastery grew up which is referred to in a charter of Louis the Pious in 816 as 'the house of the Church of St. Mewan (i.e. Méen), and St. Judicaël'. At St. Méen-le-Grand, not far from Gaël, the remains of the abbey of St. Méen are still to be seen, and the Church and the chapel of St. Méen are still visited by pilgrims. We shall see that in Britain also the Anchorite Movement is widely attested in both documentary sources and in archaeological remains.

All this extreme Eastern asceticism and its developments in western Europe may seem remote alike from the writings of St. Patrick and from the more developed forms of the Celtic Church. How has it reached Irish

[1] *Vitae Patrum*, xiv, cap. 3. On the subject of eremitism Leclercq has some salutary remarks (*Dictionnaire*, col. 385), which he concludes with the words: 'Les rares monuments que nous connaissons sur des érémites sont quatre inscriptions d'Égypte mentionnant le titre d'anachorète comme la profession du défunt' (ἀναχωρητής).

soil, and what is its earliest centre? How has it reached
Ireland from the East? It is difficult to believe that it
has been brought by the Romans, the Armenians, or the
Egyptians to whom we have rare references in such
works as the Irish *Litany of the Irish Pilgrim Saints* to be
referred to later. Nor could an institution so deeply
rooted as the Irish penitential discipline have been
established in Ireland by occasional individual pilgrims
to the great Eastern shrines.

We must postulate a strong intellectual influence
operating on our islands from the East Mediterranean,
whether directly or indirectly, possibly through Aquitaine or Spain. There can be little doubt that it was
mainly through books that knowledge came to Ireland
from the Eastern Church, and that it was through books
that they acquired their anchoritic discipline from the
East. We know from the personal letters of the fifth
century of the lively intercourse of St. Jerome and the
exchange of books with St. Augustine and other scholars of the North African Church; and we know of the
influence of the Eastern Church through Evagrius on
Cassian and on the later Roman Church through St.
Benedict. Unfortunately we have no Irish library cata-
logues for the sixth century; but we shall see in the
following chapter that the anchorite tradition was one
of considerable intellectual activity, and that from the
records which they have left us their closest affinities
would seem to be with the eastern tradition and discipline. We have seen reason to believe that our islands,
and more especially Ireland, were not wholly cut off
from the intellectual fellowship of the Continent in
the fifth and sixth centuries. We shall see that early in
the seventh century Cummian, probably the abbot of

Durrow, visited Rome on two occasions connected with church organization, for the purpose of obtaining and consulting books.

It may well be that in the future the wealth of sculpture and manuscript illumination in Ireland will enable us to draw a closer link with the East Mediterranean, especially the Coptic and Syrian areas. The direct relationship of early Irish[1] and Northumbrian art with these areas is beyond question, and is unaffected by questions of the priority and the interrelationship of the two areas, though the controversy for priority in art forms has stimulated a vigorous comparison between related English and Irish manuscripts, and a new and more scientific analysis of art technique, actively carried on by such experts as Clapham,[2] Friend,[3] Masai,[4] Åberg,[5] Nordenfalk,[6] and Mlle Françoise Henry.[7] For us the most important results of the pronouncements of all these art historians are that the Celtic manuscripts of this early period exhibit art forms wholly independent of Merovingian style, and closely related to those of Coptic and Syrian manuscripts; that certain individual features are found also in somewhat later Spanish

---

[1] Lowe dates the earliest Irish manuscript, the *Cathach*, traditionally attributed to St. Columba, to this period, and refers to it as 'the pure milk of early Irish majuscule calligraphy', *Codices Latini Antiquiores*, Part ii (Oxford, 1935), no. 266; cf. p. xii.

[2] *Antiquity*, 1934.

[3] 'The Canon Tables of the Book of Kells', *Medieval Studies in Memory of A. Kingsley Porter*, ii (Harvard, 1939), pp. 611 ff.

[4] *Essai sur les origines de la miniature dite irlandaise* (Brussels, 1947).

[5] *The Occident and the Orient in the Art of the Seventh Century* (Stockholm, 1943–7).

[6] 'Before the Book of Durrow', *Acta Archaeologica*, xvii (1946), pp. 141 ff.

[7] 'The Beginnings of Irish Miniature', *Gazette des Beaux-Arts*, 6th series, xxxvii (1950), pp. 145 ff. Cf. her *Irish Art in the Early Christian Period*[2] (London, 1947), pp. 60 ff.

manuscripts though unknown elsewhere;[1] and that certain of these early features of manuscript illumination are found also on the crosses of Carndonagh and Fahan Mura in the north of Ireland, the latter also bearing a Greek inscription identical in wording with that of the Trinitarian Spanish Mozarabic orthodoxy sanctioned at the Council of Toledo in 633,[2] which, if the inscription is genuine, hints at a possible connexion between the Spanish and the Irish Churches.[3] New scientific techniques in regard to the whole subject of manuscript preparation and illumination make discussion of close interrelationship premature and irrelevant at the present stage.[4] Nevertheless, the knowledge which we already possess warrants confidence in the Eastern origin of many of the earliest Celtic manuscript illumination models and other art styles.

We have little reliable specific evidence for direct intercourse between east Mediterranean lands and Great Britain during this period, and though it is reasonably certain that voyages were made for purposes of trade[5] it is unthinkable that these can have had any important effect on the Christianity of the West. It has been suggested on the grounds of a gloss in the twelfth-

[1] See A. M. Friend, loc. cit.

[2] R. A. S. Macalister, *Corpus Inscriptionum Insularum Celticarum*, ii (Dublin, 1949), no. 951.

[3] Nordenfalk, op. cit., p. 170.

[4] For a valuable summary of the position see the review by R. L. S. Bruce-Mitford of *Early Christian Art in Ireland* by M. and L. de Paor, in *Medieval Archaeology*, ii (1958), pp. 214 ff. I am indebted to Dr. Bertram Colgrave for calling my attention to this important note.

[5] One interesting instance occurs in the Life of St. John the Almsgiver, Patriarch of Alexandria, cap. 10, written by his disciple Leontius in the first half of the seventh century, in which a ship is stated to carry corn from Alexandria, bringing back a freight of tin (see Dawes and Baynes, *Three Byzantine Saints*, p. 217).

century manuscript of the Leiden Glossary[1] that there
was probably a specially close correspondence between
Aquitaine and southern Ireland in the fifth century.
Without placing undue weight on this single and perhaps slightly ambiguous gloss, it is in fact highly probable that refugees from this area may have made their
way to Ireland as a result of the Barbarian Invasions,
taking with them their culture and the last echoes of
classical learning, perhaps also some of the newer influences in church liturgy and hymns and their metres.
We are in fact not without hints that western Britain
and southern Ireland shared the literary culture of
Aquitaine at this period. In particular there are indica-
tions that southern Ireland was in active communication with the outside world, especially Aquitaine and
North Africa. One of the most important centres of
this communication was undoubtedly the monastery of
Lismore on the Blackwater in Munster. I hope in the
following lecture to show reasons for believing that this
monastery, together with that of Tallaght in Leinster,
was an important centre of the earliest anchorite movement in Ireland. In the meantime I will conclude this
present lecture with a brief reference to some of the
cultural influences entering Ireland from the Mediterranean areas and south-western Europe at this time.

Lismore was itself an important centre of wide culture
and learning by the standards of the time. It was in
active communication with the outside world. Père
Grosjean, Bollandist, has brilliantly demonstrated that
the address to the clergy of certain monasteries contained
in the *De Mirabilibus* attributed to St. Augustine and

[1] An English translation of the gloss in question is given by Kuno
Meyer in *Learning in Ireland in the Fifth Century and the Transmission of
Letters* (Dublin, 1913), p. 4.

associated with Carthage in North Africa refers in reality not to Carthage but to Carthy (L. *Carthagum*), i.e. the monastery of St. Carthach, the founder of Lismore (cf. p. 75 below). And further by Père Grosjean's identification of other peace-names in the document he has shown that it was written in the mid-seventh century, and was a partaker in a literary fashion of south-western Gaul and northern Spain still at this time under Visigothic rule. By this literary affectation scholars wrote under the assumed names of famous literary men. It was a kind of literary game without the slightest intention of deceiving anyone.[1]

An outstanding example of this fashion was the grammarian, Virgilius Maro *grammaticus*,[2] who lived apparently in the closing years of the sixth and the opening years of the seventh century under the Visigothic rule in the south-western part of Gaul, perhaps near Toulouse or in the Province of Navarre in Spain, where a bizarre but not wholly lifeless literary, or more properly pseudo-scholarly, life flourished somewhat ingloriously at this period. Ennodius, the bishop of Pavia (474–521), the contemporary of Virgilius, contemptuously refers to him as a *fatuus homunculus*, for usurping so honourable a name; but these literary noms-de-plume are common and were cultivated later at the Court of Charlemagne, and are probably responsible for some of the so-called forgeries. For us the importance of Virgilius lies in his evident acquaintance in some degree

[1] 'Sur quelques exégètes irlandais du VII siècle', *Sacris Erudiri*, vii (1955), pp. 67–98.
[2] For an illuminating account of Virgilius and his milieu, see K. Meyer, *Learning in Ireland in the Fifth Century* (Dublin, 1913), pp. 6 ff.; and more recently Kenney, op. cit., pp. 143 ff., and the references there cited. See especially G. Calder, *Auraicept na n-Éces* (Edinburgh, 1917), pp. xl–xliv.

with Ireland, whether from personal experience or through intermediaries. He knew something of the structure of the Irish language,[1] and of Irish tribal and personal names. His writings must have been preserved in Ireland, for they have come down to us only in manuscripts derived from an archetype in Irish script and they had considerable vogue in Ireland. They were used by the Hiberno-Latin grammarians, and had a considerable influence on works in the Irish language.[2] It is not impossible that Virgilius may have migrated to Ireland among the 'omnes sapientes cismarini' of whom it is said in the famous gloss in the Leiden MS. referred to above that they 'fugam ceperunt, et in transmarinis, videlicet in Hiberia et quocumque se receperunt, maximum profectum sapientiae incolis illarum regionum adhibuerunt'.[3]

But even if we accept the reading of *Hibernia* for the *Hiberia* of our text—a natural and legitimate expansion—there was evidently a lively intercourse between Ireland and the Visigothic kingdom in Aquitaine and northern Spain at this time, as we shall see. By far the most interesting product of this or some other similar School of linguistic bizarrerie is that strange rhetorical work the *Hisperica Famina*,[4] 'Western Sayings', dating

[1] Apparently also of Basque.
[2] Calder, loc. cit. [3] See Kuno Meyer, op. cit., p. 5.
[4] Edited by F. J. H. Jenkinson (Cambridge, 1908). For some account of the content and style, see M. L. W. Laistner, *Thought and Letters in Western Europe A.D. 500–900*[2] (London, 1957), p. 137. Kenney's account (op. cit., pp. 255 ff.) is particularly good and helpful. On the diction and Latinity, see E. K. Rand, in *Ehrengabe für K. Strecker* (Dresden, 1931), pp. 134 ff.; and for a new interpretation of the first part of the work, see P. W. Damon, in the *American Journal of Philology*, iv (1953), pp. 384 ff. Damon regards the first five capita, II. 1–132, as a dialogue between an expert rhetorician and a would-be student.

from the sixth century, with a vocabulary almost totally
artificial and largely incomprehensible, yet introducing
us to scenes among an educated, or rather a pedagogic
milieu among the *Scottigeni*, in which models extolled
are the *sophiae arcatores* and their School, perhaps rhetors,
while the contents as a whole, so far as we can interpret them, seem to offer the routine in the pupils' day.
Scholars now seem generally to be agreed that the work
was composed in Ireland, but in a milieu much like that
in Visigothic Aquitaine of the period, from where it had
doubtless had its initial inspiration.

Aquitaine is not, however, the only route by which
influences from the East by way of western Europe
may have reached southern Ireland at an early date.
Kenney was aware that Spain, together with Gaul, had
a dominant share in the transmission of European influences to Ireland,[1] and already in the early fifth century Orosius, himself a Spaniard, speaks[2] of a town which
he calls Brigantia situated in Galicia in north-western
Spain and which he evidently thinks of in some kind
of relationship to Ireland. The literary evidence is
particularly interesting. Dr. Hillgarth has assembled
some impressive evidence in a forthcoming article to
which he has given me permission to refer,[3] in which
he argues that Spain was undoubtedly an important
intermediary, both of artistic and literary influences, at
least from the middle of the seventh century, and perhaps even before 600. Among works transmitted from
Spain to Ireland at this time he cites as a probable

[1] Op. cit., pp. 139 f. (and cf. n. 100), 150, n. 136.
[2] Book I, cap. ii.
[3] A paper entitled 'The East, Visigothic Spain, and the Irish', in
Studia Patristica, vol. iv, ed. F. L. Cross (*T.U.* Bd. 79, Berlin, 1961).

instance *Theodore of Mopsuestia* translated into Latin in North Africa about this time. A clearer case can be made for the *Disticha Catonis*, and also the *Libellus ad Gregoriam*, and certain fragments from a lost work by Lactantius, found in an Irish manuscript at Milan. The work of Eugenius was already known in Ireland at this early date, and also possibly the *Ars Grammatica* perhaps by Julian of Toledo, written before 690 and read by Aldhelm and perhaps Bede.[1] The early circulation and wide influence enjoyed by Isidore of Seville in Ireland[2] might be accounted for if, as some think, the earliest manuscript tradition is Irish. It has been shown that the Victorian Easter tables, which had reached Ireland at an early date, were revised and superseded in Africa and passed through Spain, where the collection was augmented and revised, and whence it reached Ireland before 633.[3]

We have already noted the devotion with which the psalmody and the liturgy were developed in Jerusalem under Juvenal, and under St. Sabas of Judaea. This stress on the music and chanting characteristic of the Eastern Church, which is undoubtedly one of its chief gifts to the Western Church, was transmitted to Spain during the Visigothic period, and Capelle has shown reason to think that the transmission of the practice of singing the *Credo* at Mass came from the East to Spain and passed from Spain to Ireland, and only thence to England. 'À l'Âge d'Or de l'influence visigothique

---

[1] See further J. Hillgarth, *Journal of the Warburg and Courtauld Institutes* (1958), pp. 7–26, and the references there cited.

[2] Cf., for example, for his immediate influence on grammarians, G. Calder, *Auraicept na n-Éces*, pp. xxxi ff.

[3] C. W. Jones, *Baedae Opera de Temporibus* (Cambridge, Mass., 1943), pp. 65 f., 76 f., 97, 105, 112 ff.

l'Irlande curieuse et fantaisiste emprunta donc beau-
coup, et directement à l'Espagne.'[1]

The routes by which various forms of culture may
have been passed through the intellectual centres of
Spain to Ireland are many, but Galicia must surely have
been one of them, at least in the late sixth and early
seventh centuries. This is an ancient Celtic area in
which the Suevi had established themselves early in the
Migration Period, doubtless by sea,[2] and this old Suevic
kingdom was not destroyed by the Visigoths till 585,
and still continued to possess a considerable amount of
independence throughout our period. It was, moreover,
a Catholic State, while the Visigoths were Arians. It is,
therefore, initially not surprising to find that the monasticism of Galicia differed in many ways from that of
most of Spain.

A special link must in any case have existed between
the Celtic world and the Celtic monastery of Santa
Maria de Bretoña, Pastoriza, near Mondoñedo in
the northern part of Galicia, which under the title of
monasterium Maximi, is referred to, together with
churches in the Asturias, as included in the episcopate
of *Britonia* in a list which appears to be a genuine
record from Suevic times.[3] Many early Galician customs
are conservative, for example, their tardy acceptance

[1] D. Capelle, 'Alcuin et l'histoire du symbole de la messe', *Recherches
de théologie ancienne et médiévale*, vi (1934), pp. 249 ff.

[2] See R. L. Reynolds, 'Reconsideration of the History of the Suevi',
Revue belge de philologie et d'histoire, xxxv (1957), pp. 19 ff.

[3] For the text and its authenticity, see P. David, *Études historiques sur
la Galice et le Portugal* (Paris, 1947), especially pp. 1 ff., 19 ff., 57 ff.
The entry in the *Divisio Theodemiri* in which the list occurs is as follows (ibid., p. 44): 'XIII. 1. Ad sedem Britonorum ecclesias que
sunt intro Britones una cum monasterio Maximi et que in Asturiis
sunt.'

of the Vulgate,[1] the 'probably Irish-inspired penitential system', and the ascetic organization in small monastic groups hardly modified by the introduction of cenobitism by Martin of Braga c. 550 till the wider influence of St. Fructuosus in the following century.[2] The organization[3] seems to be wholly that of the Celtic Church as we know it elsewhere, and the Celtic signature of their bishop Mailoc appears as *Britonensis Ecclesiae episcopus* endorsing the acts of the Council of Braga in 572.[4] In fact an important monastery is attested here from 561–675, and the see of Britoña—not, however, wholly independent—till 830, when it was merged in the see of Mondoñedo. It may be added that seventh-century Galicia appears to have had a rich literary tradition.[5] We have already seen that in the early fifth century Orosius speaks of a city in Galicia which he calls *Brigantia*, and which he clearly regards as enjoying some kind of relations with Ireland.

While much remains uncertain, and the origin of Christianity in our islands must still remain unknown, it seems reasonably clear that there were Christian communities in Britain in the days of Tertullian and Origen, and that in Ireland there were well-established communities before the fifth century—before, that is to say, the mission of Palladius or of Patrick. The evidence suggests that in Britain, at least in northern and western Britain, Christianity had a continuous history from

---

[1] C. J. Bishko, 'The Date and Nature of the Spanish *Consensoria Monachorum*', *American Journal of Philology*, lxix (1948), p. 384.

[2] Ibid., pp. 392 ff.

[3] For an account of this, see David, op. cit., pp. 57 ff.

[4] Bishko, op. cit., p. 394; id., *Speculum*, xxiii (1948), p. 581.

[5] Id., 'The Date and Nature of the Spanish *Consensoria Monachorum*', *American Journal of Philology*, lxix. 388 f.

Roman times. Our surviving documents lead us to conclude that from one of these British Christian communities, perhaps in Strathclyde or the Solway area, St. Patrick received a call to convert the Irish; and that, having received consecration as a bishop, he established the Roman form of Christianity in the northern part of the island, essentially in the territory of Uí Néill. For the early history of Christianity in Ireland apart from St. Patrick's *paruchia* we have little direct evidence. On the whole, however, we have reason to believe that it was widespread before the coming of St. Patrick; that it had reached southern Ireland from the Mediterranean areas, perhaps through Aquitaine and Spain; and that it was well established at an early date. Already in the traditions of the sixth century Ireland comes before us as an Island of Saints (*sancti*), thickly studded with anchoritic and monastic settlements, and, as I hope to indicate, as the outermost ripple of the great monastic movement of the Greek and Coptic Churches of the East.

II

THE AGE OF THE SAINTS IN
THE CELTIC CHURCH

Hibernia insula Scotorum sanctis viris plena habetur (MARIANUS
SCOTUS in anno 674)

PASSING from the fifth century to the sixth in Ireland
is like passing from the modern world to the Desert
Fathers. The *Letter* and the *Confession* which claim to
be by St. Patrick, despite their schoolboy Latinity and
all their crabbed style and formlessness, belong to the
same world as that of his contemporaries in Gaul. The
level of thought and the manner of expression speak to
us directly. No interpreter is needed. Even his humility
has a modern ring. It is the humility which must be
felt by all men in the face of the great mystery behind
the revealed Universe, rather than the professional
humility expressed in a regular formula by the professed
religious of the monastic Orders. We of today share
Patrick's balanced outlook, his realism, his insistence
on the present world in which we live, and the necessity of the Christian to formulate his standards and con-
duct with direct relationship to his environment and his
fellow men.

But turning from the fifth century to the sixth we feel
ourselves in a different world. We lose the guidance of
contemporary documents, of course, but so far as we can
judge by those of the period immediately succeeding,
the spiritual atmosphere has become more intense. We

seem to be remote from the balanced outlook of the
Roman Church, where the environment is conditioned
by the framework of the Roman civil state. We now
lose touch with familiar Christian figures like Ausonius,
and Sidonius, and Patrick himself. In the saints of the
sixth century the standards appear to be exclusively
spiritual: the worshipper aims, not at Christian activity,
but at contemplation. The training is severe, and follows a carefully graded ascetic discipline. The saint's
terms of reference are dictated, not by episcopal authority in a Roman framework, but by the personal spiritual adviser, the *anmchara* (Irish) or *periglour* (Welsh)
of each individual saint, who in his turn is following a different tradition. Are these isolated experi-
mentalists, or are they, too, working in an historical
tradition? It will be our concern to try to trace the
origin of this sixth-century tradition of sanctity, and
to define more closely the course by which it may have
reached the Western Islands.

Two matters of outstanding importance must be
borne in mind at the outset. The sixth century is the
period to which traditions trace the rise of the great
monasteries. It is to these monasteries that we owe
almost all our written evidence for this period. We must
not be surprised, therefore, if they are silent on traditions of the Church believed to have been founded by
St. Patrick; and also on other kinds of foundations, such
as privately owned churches,[1] which were not strictly
monastic in origin. We can learn something of these
churches incidentally; but the direct information left

[1] For a lucid general definition of privately owned churches during
the fourth and fifth centuries, see P. David, *Études historiques sur la Galice
et le Portugal du VIᵉ au XIIᵉ siècle* (Paris, 1947), pp. 9 ff.

us by the monastic writers naturally relates almost exclusively to the saints and the monastic foundations attributed to them, and may give us a disproportionate view of their exclusive importance. We have to bear in mind that privately owned churches certainly existed, both in Ireland and in Wales,[1] and also in early times in England.[2]

It is perhaps in connexion with such privately owned churches that the origin of the system known as the *co-arbship* is to be most readily understood. This is one of the most interesting and characteristic institutions of the Celtic Church, not only in Ireland, but also in Scotland, and to some extent in Wales. Stated in its simplest terms, land granted by a chief to a saint was a personal grant to himself and his heirs, who were originally[3] drawn from the kindred of the original founder, and who became his 'heirs', 'inheritors', *com-arbae*. The story of the foundation of the church of Armagh by the gift of Daire to St. Patrick, as related by Muirchu in his *Life* of the saint (cap. 24), is a typical illustration of the institution, both in its origin and in the succession of its incumbents. The co-arbs of Patrick, preserved in the diptychs or ecclesiastical lists of Armagh, suggest that till the middle of the sixth century Armagh was an episcopal see which then became a monastic church. During two following centuries the abbots also held the office of bishops. The list of succession of various Irish churches, such as Trim; Bangor, Co. Down; Nendrum;

---

[1] For some interesting details of these private chapels, see Sir J. E. Lloyd, *History of Wales*, i. 218 f.

[2] See W. Levison, *Relations between England and the Continent in the eighth century* (Oxford, 1946), pp. 28 f. and references.

[3] For a study of the system and its later developments see J. Barry, *Irish Ecclesiastical Record*, 5th series, lxxxix (1958), 24 ff., 424 ff.

and even the new Danish bishopric of Dublin,[1] illustrate the system of the co-arbship very well, and in Scotland the succession of Iona is especially instructive. The working of the co-arbship is also clearly illustrated in the succession to the nunnery of Killeevy in Co. Armagh, founded by St. Darerca or Moninna,[2] whose extant Life, written in the ninth century, is believed to be based on one written in the first half of the seventh century, and therefore to be one of the oldest.[3] She is represented as a contemporary of St. Brigit, and her death is entered in the Annals of Ulster in 517. A short list[4] of the succession of her abbesses at Killeevy, found in the manuscript in the British Museum which contains her life, gives her own successors from the fifth to the fifteenth abbess, and is very instructive. The thirteenth abbess was the daughter of Foidmenn, king of Conaille Muirthemne around Dundalk, in which Killeevy lay. His sister and daughter were successively abbesses here. The eighth abbess was granddaughter of the fifth, and the ninth and tenth were sisters, nieces of the eighth.

The second important matter to be borne in mind is that the Celtic Church was never outside the framework of the Roman Church. I stressed in my last lecture that all our testimony for both Britain and Ireland suggests that the Celtic Church was in all respects at one with the established episcopal Church of Gaul at this

[1] See J. Conway Davies, *Episcopal Acts relating to Welsh Dioceses*, ii (published by the Historical Society of the Church in Wales, 1948), pp. 463 f.

[2] A full account of her is given by the Rev. J. Ryan, S.J., *Irish Monasticism* (Dublin 1931), pp. 136 f.

[3] See Esposito, 'The Sources of Conchubranus' Life of St. Moninna', *English Historical Review*, xxxv (1920), pp. 71 ff.

[4] Edited by Esposito, *Proceedings of the Royal Irish Academy*, xxviii (1910), pp. 244 f.

period. The so-called 'Celtic Church' was still fundamentally one with the Continental Church, which looked in the earliest days to the ecclesiastical prestige, and later to the authority of Rome as its head. It held the same faith, was founded on the same Christian tradition, and had the same hope of the Resurrection. It was completely orthodox. Owing to its remote position it suffered from irregular contact with the continental institutions and thought during the Barbarian invasions. Consequently it clung to certain early practices in matters of ritual which had prevailed in the early Continental Church, but had been superseded with the passage of time; but indeed in these early days the Continental Church was by no means uniform in its practice. Uniformity was only achieved very gradually.[1]

Local conditions within the Celtic countries also continued to produce very considerable modifications in the economy of the Church and its form of local establishments; and the predominance of the monastic foundations in the life of the Church in the Celtic countries developed differences, both of organization and of ritual, from those of the Continental Church. This divergence became a matter of growing bitterness and misunderstanding at the time, and lasted into the eighth century, and often resulted in accusations of separatism and even of heresy, though the charges were never substantiated and were certainly unjust. Those who, like Bede, looked to the authority of Canterbury as the representative of Rome in our islands had no sympathy with, or understanding of, the Celtic Church whose members refused to accept this Canterbury

[1] See Dom Morin, *Revue bénédictine*, viii (1891), p. 97.

authority, and clung to the traditions of the Church which they had received from earlier days. But there was no theological difference or doctrinal separation from the Church of the Continent, nothing sectarian, nothing unorthodox. We shall see that when St. Augustine from Rome and Canterbury met the British bishops in council he met them as colleagues, not as heretics. We shall see that when the popes wrote letters to the Celtic Church on the Easter dispute, they wrote as to members of their own Church. At the Council of Whitby in 663, which we may look upon as the closing date of the Celtic Church in Northumbria, the issue was debated, not on any point of doctrine, but on the reformed continental dating of the Easter Festival.

The Celtic practices then which were regarded by the Roman Church of the period as irregular were not new or provincial institutions, but in some measure out-of-date practices retained in a backward region on the periphery of the Continental Church at a date later than that in which they had been in use in various parts of the Continent. These can be traced in their fullest development in the Irish Church, though they are shared in varying degrees also by the Welsh Church in Britain (both Wales and apparently Strathclyde) and in Brittany, and the Columban Church, which is, of course, Irish in origin, and indeed by all the Celtic communities on the Continent also.

In a study of the literary and historical aspects of the Celtic Church any detailed account of the points of ritual in which variations from the continental practice had developed would be out of place, but a few of the more important points may be referred to here, more especially as the questions frequently asked by modern churchmen suggest that the matter is one of considerable interest even to people today.

Among the matters of outstanding importance is the question of the baptismal rite, on which there seems to have been considerable difference. Bede (*Eccles. Hist.* ii. 2) refers to some defect, but its nature is not quite clear—possibly single immersion,[1] which was a Breton custom till 1620, and prevailed also in sixth-century Spain, where there was probably a Breton bishopric at the time. The earliest Anglo-Saxon decrees provide for the invocation of each person of the Trinity in baptism, which implies the observance of the Apostolic Canon commanding trine immersion. The later Irish seem to have omitted chrism, to judge by Lanfranc's letter of 1074 to Turlough O'Brien.

Other special features are:

1. Some peculiarities in the liturgy and ritual of the Mass, the Celtic being closer to the Gallican usage than to the Roman,[2] e.g. the multiplicity of the Collects in the Columban Church in the seventh century, perhaps shared with the British Church also.[3]

Both southern Gaul and Milan have been suggested as the source of some peculiarities in the usage of the Gallican Church. Le P. J.-B. Thibaut, in a very full and careful examination of the evidence, favours Lérins[4] and the monastery of Saint-Victor at Marseilles as the source.

2. A number of rites relating to ordination, perhaps British in origin, are claimed as peculiar to the early Northumbrian and probably Scottish Churches.

[1] Haddan and Stubbs, *Councils*, i. 153.
[2] F. E. Warren, *The Liturgy and Ritual of the Celtic Church* (Oxford, 1881), p. 75.
[3] Haddan and Stubbs, *Councils*, i. 154.
[4] See Le P. J.-B. Thibaut, *L'Ancienne Liturgie gallicane* (Paris, 1929).

3. Perhaps the most debated point in the Celtic usage is that of the consecration of a bishop by a single bishop. Without entering into a detailed discussion here it must be pointed out that despite the statement and instances of both Haddan and Stubbs[1] and Conway Davies[2] there is no reliable evidence that this was ever a practice of the Celtic Church. All the instances adduced are late and unreliable, and Owen Chadwick has shown that the only early instance—that in the Life of St. Samson —rests on a misinterpretation of the text.[3] Warren[4] called attention to the fact that three British bishops had been present at the Council of Arles in 314 which ordered that at least three, and if possible seven, bishops should take part in every episcopal consecration.

Among the *Responsiones* attributed to Gregory the Great in answer to questions put to him by St. Augustine of Canterbury is that of permission for ordination by a single bishop when it was found difficult or impossible to get three bishops present.

Nevertheless, the important fact remains that Archbishop Theodore saw some flaw in Celtic ordination which made him suspect the imperfection of the Celtic orders,[5] and think it necessary to confirm the consecration of Chad to the episcopal see. His consecration had been performed by Wini, bishop of Winchester, assisted by two British bishops, A.D. 665 (Bede, iii. 28), but was apparently held invalid (ibid. iv. 2).

[1] *Councils*, i. 155.
[2] *Episcopal Acts relating to the Welsh Dioceses*, ii (1948), p. 485.
[3] In *Studies in Early British History* (ed. N. K. Chadwick), pp. 173 ff.
[4] Op. cit., p. 69.
[5] In Theodore's *Penitential* (II. ix) we read: 'Qui ordinati sunt a Scottorum vel Britonum episcopis . . . adunati ecclesiae non sunt, sed iterum a catholico episcopo manus impositione confirmentur' (Warren, op. cit., p. 68, n. 6).

Other variations also existed, e.g. in the mode of consecrating churches and monasteries. Perhaps the most interesting of the differences as a whole is that of the list of the Orders of the hierarchy of the Church, in which the British Church seems to have preserved, not the Orders of the *Statuta antiqua Ecclesiae* of Leo the Great adopted at Arles, but the earlier ones of the period of the Bishops Rusticus of Narbonne and Venerius of Marseilles (*c.*431–51) and the young Faustus, at this time a monk of Lérins.[1] It would seem probable from what Dom. Morin says on this matter[2] that not only the Orders of the Church, but the baptismal rite also was involved in this early corresponding usage between Britain and Gaul.

Nevertheless, it must always be borne in mind that there was no fundamental divergence of church ritual. The bishop was always the leading member of the church hierarchy, and he alone was qualified to consecrate other bishops and churches and cemeteries. No abbot had this right, unless, as sometimes happened, he was also a bishop. The succession of the church hierarchy through priests and deacons and the lower orders was maintained. It is only in a general sense that we are justified in speaking of a 'Celtic Church', because while the Celtic Church had come to differ from the Continental Roman Church in many details of practice, yet within the Celtic lands, with their conservative usage, considerable uniformity prevailed, despite some local variations which had developed in the course of time.

[1] The evidence is furnished by an extant letter of south-eastern Gaul addressed to Bishop Rusticus of Narbonne, and attributed to Faustus of Riez, while he was still a monk of Lérins. See the very interesting article by Dom Morin, *Revue bénédictine*, viii (1891), p. 97.

[2] Loc. cit.

The most outstanding feature of this Celtic Church was the widespread extent and power of the monastic foundations. By the sixth century these had come to give it an individual character and local tradition to which it clung passionately in the face of attempts from Rome and Canterbury to bring it into full conformity with continental usages. Our documents are fullest for Ireland and also for the so-called 'Columban Church' of Scotland, and the earliest Northumbrian Church, both of which owe their origins to the Irish Church of this period. Wales and Brittany also formed important areas of the Celtic Church, and Wales in particular clung tenaciously to her old traditions long after the other Celtic countries had joined the Roman Order.

The Breton Church, founded in the early days of the colonization of Brittany in the fifth and sixth centuries, chiefly from south Wales, has preserved many valuable traditions of her early Church. Although Breton sources are for the most part late, they include our earliest *vitae* of Welsh saints, and they are particularly valuable because we know a considerable amount of the Roman Order of the Church in a large part of Brittany, and are able to trace the relationship between the native Roman and the incoming British institutions. Nor must we forget the Isle of Man; for although we are unfortunately without early written records for the history of the island, tradition assigns its conversion to an early date, and the wealth of early crosses and inscriptions, and the tiny Christian *keeills*, 'oratories' or 'chapels'—over two hundred in number—show a closer concentration of early Christian remains than those of any area of comparable size in the British Isles. The linguistic and material remains of Manx Christianity show it as partaking for the most part with the Christianity of Ireland in the earliest period, and perhaps throughout the Viking Age. Nevertheless, by far the greater part of our written evidence for the Celtic Church has reference to Ireland and to the Columban and Northumbrian Churches to which she gave birth, and it is most usually of Ireland that we think when we speak in general terms of the 'Celtic Church'.

For the right understanding of the Church of the Celtic countries during its special period, the sixth century, the period when it first comes before us as 'The Age of the Saints', and the following century, it is important to consider a work which was long held to be an authentic document of the eighth century and which gives an analysis of the principal elements of the early Irish Church. This document is the famous *Catalogus Sanctorum Hiberniae*, the 'Catalogue of the Saints of Ireland'.[1] In this it is stated that the Orders of the Saints of Ireland were three in number, to which, in certain manuscripts, a relative chronology is assigned.

The First Order, which is described as 'most holy', were those who received their *missa*, their 'order of services', from St. Patrick. In this Order, we are told, all the saints were bishops. There was unity in the Church, and one liturgy only. They did not reject the fellowship and ministration of women.

Here we note the central organization on the principle of the continuous episcopal organization of the

---

[1] Printed in Haddan and Stubbs, *Councils*, II. ii. 292 f. Cf. Bury, *St. Patrick* (London, 1905), pp. 285 ff. The study of the *Catalogus* by the Rev. Paul Grosjean, Bollandiste, has superseded all earlier studies. See 'Édition et commentaire du Catalogus Sanctorum Hiberniae', *Analecta Bollandiana*, lxxiii (1955).

Church of the Continent, and the stress throughout on unity.

The *Second Order*, which is here said to be only 'very holy', and which is apparently conceived as succeeding the first, consisted mainly, not of bishops, of whom there are categorically stated to have been very few, but of presbyters. They had varied liturgies and various monastic rules. They refused the ministration of women, who were separated from the monasteries. They received their Order (*missam acceperunt*) from the holy men of Britain, SS. David, Gildas, and Docus.

The *Third Order* is described as merely 'holy', and as dwelling in desert places, living on herbs and water and alms, and possessing nothing of their own.

The bias of the document is clear. It is composed as an element in the great controversy between the Roman and the monastic Church, to be considered more fully in my final lecture, and it is clearly conceived in the interests of the Church of St. Patrick at Armagh. The Second Order is treated as inferior to the First, and the Third Order clearly refers to the so-called Anchorite or Culdee movement, generally regarded by modern scholars as a 'reform'. Its members were ascetic and solitary, not isolated, but withdrawn from the fuller community. Yet it seems to have been bound up with a great literary activity, and it numbered among its devotees some of the greatest poets and intellectual monks of early Ireland, such as Oengus the Culdee.

It is this document, which claims to be contemporary with the Third Order of Saints, that is largely responsible for the view that this Order is later than the First or Second Order, and that it is in fact a reform movement arising from the Second Order, and subsequent to it. It has been shown by the Bollandist scholar, the Rev. Paul Grosjean,[1] however, that the document is not earlier than the ninth or even the tenth century; that it already shows an imperfect knowledge of the Third Order; and that its information, far from being first-hand and contemporary, is derived from earlier written sources. If we can disabuse our minds of the spurious authority of the *Catalogus* and look to the records of the early Irish Church, I think it becomes clear that the so-called Third Order has always been an integral part of the monastic Church; that there is little ground for regarding the religious of this Order as constituting a 'Reform'; and that the literary movement with which they are associated is not the expression of a new development, but the formulation in writing of their early traditional beliefs and discipline. The eremetical life in Egypt or Syria does not there appear to be a reform, or successor to the coenobitic life, or at least to the general monastic life of the *lavra*, but an accompaniment of it, an element in it. Our Irish anchorites and scribes, the members of the Third Order, to employ the convenient classification of the *Catalogus*, seem to hold a similar position. It is largely the failure to recognize this which is responsible for the difficulty felt by all scholars who have sought to define the Anchorites and Culdees as distinct elements in the organization of the Celtic Church.

The *Catalogus* derived the Second Order from Britons, stating that they received their *missa*, or order of services, from Bishops David, Gildas, and Docus. Gildas is in all probability 'Gildas *auctor*' referred to by St. Columbanus in a letter to Pope Gregory the Great as one whose

[1] Op. cit., pp. 197 ff., 292 ff.

F

advice was sought on a matter of church discipline by
a certain Vennianus *auctor*, presumably from his name
an Irishman (Finnian, perhaps of Clonard, or possibly
Moville), and the reference suggests that he was a person of some authority in church matters. Docus has not
been identified, and I have tried to show elsewhere[1]
that we have no evidence that St. David's importance
in Wales was of so early a date. The tradition of the
Catalogus regarding the part played by these saints in
the foundation of Irish monasticism is late and spurious,
though it is possible that some form of the *missa* may have
been transmitted from Britain at this time. It is commonly held that the forms of certain ecclesiastical loan-
words introduced into Irish from Latin can best be
explained by supposing them to have come through a
British medium[2] (cf. p. 11 above).

It is the form of Irish Christianity which the *Catalogus*
has called the Second Order which differentiates it from
the Patrician Church, and which is the fundamental
element of the 'Age of the Saints' in the sixth century.
Its origin is essentially a personal one, the names and
acta of a large number of saintly founders being assigned
to this period, first by the consistent testimony of tradition, and later by an equally consistent body of written
records. The traditional founder of this great monastic
movement in Ireland was St. Finnian of Clonard, whose
death, according to the *Annals of Ulster*, took place in
548 (*recte* 549).[3]

---

[1] *Studies in the Early British Church* (Cambridge, 1958), pp. 121 ff.

[2] H. Zimmer, *The Early Celtic Church* (English translation by A. Meyer,
London, 1902), pp. 24 f. For a valuable recent discussion on this subject,
see K. H. Jackson, *Language and History in Early Britain* (Edinburgh, 1953),
pp. 122 ff.

[3] For the most recent work on his cult, see Dr. Kathleen Hughes,

The most striking feature of this Second or monastic Order is the absence of central organization. The rapid and widespread development of monasticism brought with it no uniformity. Each of the great monastic foundations exercised autonomy. Each claimed to be the creation of a saintly founder who lived about the sixth century, and to whom the community looked back as their sole authority. It is for this reason that we have a number of great independent monasteries which became famous, first for their special sanctity, and later often for their educational and literary pre-eminence, and their famous *scriptoria*. Among the most outstanding are Kildare, traditionally founded by St. Brigit; Clonmacnoise on the Shannon, founded by St. Cierán, a great home of learning and the place where the *Annals of Tigernach* were written; Clonfert, perhaps founded by that St. Brendan whose voyage is the Christian Odyssey of early Ireland; Bangor in Co. Down, founded by St. Comgall, and generally regarded as the home of the earliest historical annals. Hardly less well known, and perhaps most interesting of all, is Lismore on the River Blackwater in south-east Munster, founded by St. Carthach, otherwise known as Mochuta, of whom I have already spoken, and shall have more to say later.

These important monastic foundations were, it seems, quite independent of one another. Each might found daughter houses which apparently recognized some authority in the founding house, but it is quite likely that this would be merely one of prestige. We have reason to think that the monastery of Terryglas on

Analecta Bollandiana, lxxiv. 342 (his offices); id., *Irish Historical Studies*, ix (1954) (his cult); *English Historical Review* (1954), p. 354 ('The Historical Value of the Lives of St. Finnian of Clonard').

the Shannon owed some kind of loyalty, or possibly obedience, to the monastery of Tallaght just south of Dublin, founded by Máelruáin; but this was not until the eighth century, probably in the latter half. Whether affiliations carried with them financial or other obligagations we do not know. The monasteries of Tallaght and Finglas, to the north and south of the River Liffey near Dublin, were certainly in friendly relations with one another and were known as the 'Two Eyes of Ireland' (cf. p. 88 below.)

In medieval *vitae* these co-operative relations are described as if they were the personal friendships formed by the founding saints; but this is quite unhistorical. For example, in chapter 14 of the *Life* of St. Declán, the chief saint of the southern Dési, and the founder of the monastery of Ardmore at the mouth of the River Blackwater on the south coast of Munster, we are told that the saints 'Declán, Ailbe, and Íbar made a bond of friendship and a league amongst themselves and their spiritual posterity in heaven and on earth for ever, and they loved one another.'

This we may safely interpret as a co-operative agreement of a later period, expressed in hagiographical terms, between the monastery of Ardmore among the southern Dési, Emly, the chief church of ancient Munster, and Beggery Island in Wexford Harbour. Late traditions in the *vitae* of these saints and others of ancient Munster represent them as having introduced Christianity into Ireland before Patrick.[1] Such monastic groups, whatever their nature, do not necessarily involve even unity of usage, and we have definite evidence that there was no unity even of liturgical usage among

[1] Kenney, op. cit., p. 310.

the Irish monastic houses. In this absence of central authority, however, it is important to remember that the Celtic Church did not differ essentially from the Continental Church, in which the bishop of Rome, in the early centuries of our era, possessed no technical authority. The absence of central authority and organization based on it was undoubtedly the cause of the ultimate extinction of the Celtic Church.

In other respects also the internal organization of the Irish Church differed from that of the Continent. The position of the bishops was peculiar, and differed from that of the continental bishoprics with their urban and centralized populations. The Celtic economy, with the scattered pastoral population and absence of towns, offered no natural basis for the development of territorial sees. The duties and privileges of a Celtic bishop were exclusively of a ritual character. The bishops seem to have had their principal dwellings in the monasteries, sometimes, we are told, two or even more in one monastery. Bede's account of St. Aidan is perhaps our fullest picture of an early Celtic bishop. His principal seat seems to have been in the island of Lindisfarne, where he lived with the 'Brethren'; but as we have seen in my former lecture he travelled much, going about with the king from one of his country seats to another, and from time to time retiring to the little island of Farne two miles away for solitude and prayer. He also had a church and an apartment at the king's country seat near Bamborough, from which he could go about and preach among the country people.

There were, of course, no archbishops in the Celtic Church, and a bishop had no authority in the economy or organization of a monastery ruled by an abbot.

St. Columba was abbot of Iona, and by courtesy the head of the widest organization within the Celtic Church; but he was never a bishop, and though other churches of the Columban confederation followed the same practices as the Irish Church in this respect, Columba remained a presbyter till the end of his life.[1] When a bishop from Ireland visited Iona, Columba gave place to him in the celebration of the Lord's Supper.[2] Even in Iona the office and jurisdiction of abbot did not carry with it any of the spiritual functions of bishop, whether for the ordination of priests, or for confirmation, or for the consecration of graveyards.[3] It is possible that the Welsh episcopacy may have developed on somewhat different lines from the Irish, owing to the early urbanizing influence of the Roman Occupation: but the point is not clear, and the original relationship between the monasteries and the bishoprics in Wales is disputed.[4]

Our evidence makes it clear that the Order of the saintly founders and that of the Anchorites are not only contemporary but very closely related. In a quotation from Isidore of Seville adopted into the Irish Collection of Canons the Third Order is thus identified with both the Anchorites and also with the monastic community. 'Tertium genus est anachoretarum qui iam coenobiali conversatione perfecti semetipsos includunt in cellulis procul a conspectu hominum remotis nemini ad se prebentes accessum, sed in sola contemplatione theorica viventes perseverant.'[5]

---

[1] Bede, *H. E.* iii. 4. [2] Adamnán, *Vita S. Columbae*, i. 35. [3] Ibid. i. 29.

[4] For a recent statement of the position of the episcopate in the Celtic Church, and especially in the Church of Wales, see Conway Davies, *Episcopal Acts relating to the Welsh Dioceses*, ii (1948), pp. 470 ff.

[5] F. W. H. Wasserschleben, *Die irische Kanonensammlung*² (Leipzig, 1885), xxxix. 3, p. 148.

Great missionary activity is held to be a special character of the Irish Church, in contrast to the Welsh; but I think that 'mission' would be a better word than missionary, for there is little evidence that the Irish did much conversion outside Britain. What they did was to found monasteries on the Irish model in countries already at least nominally Christian, e.g. St. Columbanus, who founded monasteries in France, Italy, and Switzerland. St. Columba's relations with Bruide, Bede's *rex potentissimus*, king of the Northern Picts, were surely dictated by necessity if the Irish were to occupy Iona. An ancient tradition has it that the youngest member of the Irish royal family of Argyll had already been converted by St. Patrick before leaving Ireland. Presumably Columba went there to look after the Irish colonists, not to convert them. In fact we hear surprisingly little of new foundations by St. Columba. Bede tells us definitely that the arrival of the Columban monks in Northumbria was in direct response to an invitation by King Oswald, and that Northumbria had been previously converted by St. Paulinus of Canterbury. Welsh monks also emigrated in great numbers to Brittany, and it is claimed that they only ministered to the Welsh colonists, not to the Bretons. But the native Bretons already had an organized Christian Church of their own, in all respects like the Church of Gaul, and dating from the Gallo-Roman period.[1]

St. Columba, pioneer founder of island sanctuaries in Britain; St. Columbanus, conducting a kind of ecclesiastical tour through France, Switzerland, and

[1] For recent writings on this subject, see the studies by Couffon (1944), and Merlet (1950 and 1951), in *Mémoires de la Société d'Histoire et d'Archéologie de Bretagne*.

Italy, and founding monasteries and ecclesiastical centres
as he went; St. Samson, from South Wales, possibly the
greatest political force among all the Breton colonists,
and founder of the most important Breton Church—
all these are practising a very interesting and characteristic form of ascetic discipline known as *peregrinatio*,
'peregrination', 'wandering', literally 'pilgrimage'.[1]
This is something quite different from missionary work,
or even mission work. The Celtic *papas*, 'ecclesiastics',
whose croziers and bells were found at a later date in
uninhabited Iceland, had not gone to convert, but to
be 'pilgrims'. The most familiar story of a pilgrimage
of this kind is the one mentioned in the year 891 in the
Anglo-Saxon Chronicle (Parker Text), which tells how
three Irishmen came to Cornwall in a curragh, or Irish
light boat covered with skins, and without any steering
oar, 'because they wanted to go into exile for the love of
God, they cared not whither'.

As Professor Wrenn has said,[2] this is perhaps the first
Anglo-Saxon rendering of the idea of the Irish *peregrina-
tio*, though the same idea is prominent in the Anglo-
Saxon poems of the *Wanderer* and the *Seafarer*.[3]

No less impressive is the earlier account by Adamnán[4]
of the three attempts of Cormac úa Liathán, abbot
of Durrow, and also a bishop and an anchorite, to find

[1] For a general account of Welsh peregrination see E. G. Bowen, *The
Settlements of the Celtic Saints in Wales* (Cardiff, 1954).

[2] 'Saxons and Celts in south-west Britain', *The Transactions of the
Honourable Society of Cymmrodorion* (1959), p. 47.

[3] See D. Whitelock, 'The Interpretation of the *Seafarer*', in H. M.
Chadwick, *Memorial Studies in the Early Cultures of North-West Europe*
(Cambridge, 1950), pp. 261 ff.; cf. further G. V. Smithers, 'The Meaning
of the *Seafarer* and the *Wanderer*', *Medium Ævum*, xxvi (1957), pp.
137 ff.; and Ida Gordon, *The Seafarer* (London, 1960), Introduction.

[4] *Vita Columbae*, Book I, cap. 6; II, cap. 42; cf. also Reeves, op.
cit., p. 222, note e. Cormac's three voyages were apparently in process
of becoming the subject of a saga cycle.

a '*solitude*' in the Ocean, and who went astray in Arctic regions before arriving in Iona. The most famous of these voyages are, of course, the Voyages of St. Brendan to seek a Paradise in the Western Ocean,[1] while in many ways the most interesting is that of St. Colmán of Lindisfarne, who retired with his followers to the little island of Inishbófin, off the west coast of Co. Mayo, after the Council of Whitby, of which we learn from Bede,[2] and to which I shall refer more fully later.

Pilgrimage[3] in the strict sense of the term is not, of course, an exclusive characteristic of the Celtic Church. Pilgrimage as we understand the term is a movement which had its rise in the fourth century, and developed rapidly in the fifth century throughout western Christendom.[4] The rise of the great Christian centres of Rome and the East, especially Palestine, combined with facilities for travel inherited from the Roman transport organization, had given birth to a great enthusiasm for pilgrimages among both men and women, and a rich literature has come down to us claiming to be the work of *peregrini* from western lands, from Gaul, Spain, and even Britain. One of these pilgrims is described as 'sprung from the farthest shore of the western sea, the Ocean'. The records left by these *peregrini* range from personal log-books by ladies of astonishing physical

[1] See Plummer, *Lives of Irish Saints* (Oxford, 1922), i. 44 ff.
[2] *H.E.* iv, p. iv.
[3] For a general study of the theme see K. Hughes, 'The changing theory and practice of Irish Pilgrimage,' *Journal of Ecclesiastical History*, xi (1960), 143 ff.
[4] I have given some account of the early pilgrimages from western Europe to the great Christian centres, and references to the literature to which they gave rise, in *Poetry and Letters in Early Christian Gaul* (London, 1955), pp. 16 ff.

endurance and intellectual curiosity, to guide-books and technical itineraries. The earliest of all, that of the Bordeaux Pilgrim, written in 333, is a fourth-century Bradshaw, and gives a list of the principal stages in the land route from Bordeaux to the Holy Land. It is such works as these, rather than missionary enterprise, which give the background to the pilgrimage literature of the Celtic Church. In fact this is one of the principal ways in which the early Celtic Church shows itself in touch with continental thought.

Within this wider movement of pilgrimage, the distinction drawn in the so-called '*Old Irish Life of St. Columba*'[1] between various kinds of *peregrinatio* shows an awareness that there was a form which was a special ideal of the Celtic Church. This was defined in the '*Old Irish Life of St. Columba*' as 'seeking the place of one's resurrection'. This is doubtless the kind which Adamnan has in mind when he tells us that St. Columba left Ireland for Britain *pro Christo peregrinari volens enavigavit.*[2] This form of peregrination, not for travel to a famous shrine and afterwards to return, but a withdrawal from home and kindred, even from the larger religious community, to pass one's life, or a period of one's life, in solitude, is one of the most important features of early Irish asceticism, and its chief legacy to after ages.[3] It is commonly known as anchoritism, though an anchorite of the early period was not necessarily a solitary; and its close association with the great saints of the Second Order, such as St. Columba and St. Columbanus, and its more especial identification with

[1] For references see Kenney, op. cit., p. 433.
[2] *Vita S. Columbae*, Preface II.
[3] For a recent general account of the *peregrinatio* and an excellent bibliography, see E. S. Duckett, *The Wandering Saints* (London, 1959).

the solitaries and anchorites of the Third Order, is yet a further proof of the close relationship of these two Orders.

The *peregrinatio* in this specialized sense is a characteristic activity of some of the most important of the Celtic Saints. The word was interpreted in both its literal and its figurative sense. The '*Old Irish Life of St. Columba*', referred to above, which is in reality a late text of *c.* 1000, a commemorative sermon on the saint's festival, defines it thus:

God counselled Abraham to leave his own country and go in pilgrimage into the land which God had shown him, to wit, the 'Land of Promise'. . . . Now the good counsel which God enjoined here on the father of the faithful is incumbent on all the faithful; that is to leave their country and their land, their wealth and their worldly delight for the sake of the Lord of the Elements, and go in perfect pilgrimage in imitation of Him.

A little further on in the same *Life* pilgrimage is defined in three grades: The first is when a man leaves his country in body only, but with spirit still uncleansed. The second is when a man leaves his fatherland in zeal of heart, though not in body, being detained under authority in his own land, though dedicated in spirit to God. The third is when a man leaves his country altogether in body and soul, as the apostles and people of perfect pilgrimage left it. These are they of the perfect pilgrimage.[1]

It has often been stated that the monastic life was a cowardly retreat from social duty, a spiritual egotism seeking only a reward in the coming life; and that the chief motive of this peregrination of the early Celtic

[1] For references see p. 82, note 1, above; and for a translation by W. M. Hennessy, see W. F. Skene, *Celtic Scotland*, ii (Edinburgh, 1887), pp. 467 ff.

saints was the salvation of their own souls;[1] but the true
contemplative is not primarily concerned about his own
soul. The spiritual exercise of the Contemplative is defined as 'a loving attention upon God', and I think we
may accept this as the true object of pilgrimage as these
early religious of the Celtic Church understood it. As
a little poem of the Old Irish period expressed it:

> 'To go to Rome
> Is much trouble, little profit;
> The King [of Heaven] whom thou seekest there,
> Unless thou bring Him with thee, thou wilt not find.'[2]

The Anchorites, with whom are frequently mentioned the Culdees, as if they were identical or at least
closely related, are clearly the religious who in the
Catalogus are classed as the Third Order of the Saints of
Ireland. This document, as I have said already, has
been shown to date from the ninth or even the tenth
century; but it is valuable as showing the tradition
that the Anchorites were an important element in the
Church, and as giving us a picture of their way of life as
this has been handed down by tradition. Here not only
are the Third Order and the Anchorites identical, but
it is clearly stated that they represent a further stage in
the contemplative life than that of the monastic community; and in fact that the religious graduated to the
life of the Anchorite as a result of a period of preparation within the community. And this is, in fact, what we

---

[1] See, for example, Sir Samuel Dill, *Roman Society in Gaul in the Mero-
vingian Age* (London, 1926), p. 358. Cf. the Rev. J. L. G. Meissner,
'Celtic Christianity', in *The Church of Ireland, A.D. 432–1932* (Report of the
Church of Ireland Conference, Dublin, 1932), p. 79.

[2] W. Stokes and J. Strachan, *Thesaurus Palaeohibernicus*, ii. 296 (quat-
rains in the Codex Boernerianus); translated by Kuno Meyer, *Ancient
Irish Poetry*[2] (London, 1913), p. 100.

often find in certain Eastern Communities. The early Irish *Rule of the Anchorites*, which passes under the name of the *Rule of Columcille*[1] enjoins on the Anchorite to 'be alone in a desert place apart in the neighbourhood of a chief monastery if you distrust in your conscience to be in the company of many'.

This injunction is just such as guided the founders of the desert hermits of Lower Egypt and Palestine, and indeed many of Upper Egypt also. It seems, in fact, that the Anchorite life in the Celtic Church was looked upon as a degree to which only the more advanced monks might attain, and we may compare further what Bede[2] says of St. Cuthbert, who 'entered as a monk at Lindisfarne, but *crescentibus meritis religiose intentionis secreta pervenit*' on the Island of Farne, to which St. Aidan had formerly repaired at times for prayer and solitude.

The question of the relationship of the Anchorites to the monastic communities is closely bound up with that of their origin, the date of their *floruit*, and their relationship to the Culdees—all matters much disputed. The so-called Anchorite Movement is ascribed by Kenney[3] to the seventh and eighth centuries. The late Robin Flower, on the evidence of the obits in the annals, would assign it chiefly to the second half of the eighth and the whole of the ninth centuries;[4] but both these writers look upon it as a 'reform' arising as a later stage from the Age of the Saints. Flower is specific. Stressing

---

[1] For text and translation, see Haddan and Stubbs, *Councils*, (II. i. 119 ff.; translation also in W. F. Skene, *Celtic Scotland*, ii, p. 508). For further references, see Kenney, op. cit., p. 474.

[2] *H.E.* iv. 26.   [3] Op. cit., pp. 468 ff.

[4] R. Flower, 'The Two Eyes of Ireland', in *The Church of Ireland, A.D. 432–1932* (Report of the Church of Ireland Conference, Dublin, 1932), p. 72 and *passim*.

the religious activity and intellectual effort which gave it literary form he writes: 'Behind all this activity, all this multifarious production, we feel the presence of . . . the spirit that causes and sustains all reformations in religion. Reforms come about when men ask themselves with a new urgency: "How is the good life to be led?"'

I am inclined to suggest that Dr. Flower is laying too much weight on the fact that much of our evidence is conditioned by the growth of the habit of keeping annals and recording obits in the later period. To my mind all the weight of evidence is in favour of a close association of the asceticism of the Anchorites with the saints of the Second as well as the Third Order, and I believe that they were contemporary. I believe that the Revd. John Ryan, with his wider knowledge of the Christian Church as a whole, has arrived at a juster view of the date and nature of the Third Order.

Ryan describes[1] the Third Order as the general tendency to the 'desert', and ascribes it to the end of the sixth century, claiming that in Ireland it had manifested itself much earlier, and that the letter of Columbanus to Pope Gregory in the sixth century shows that it was not new in Ireland even then. Ryan brings the Anchorites into juxtaposition with the desert solitaries: and indeed it is surely impossible to believe that two institutions so similar can have developed within the Church at the same time wholly independently of one another. Yet the more fully developed forms of anchoritism in the Celtic Church do not appear to have developed from the Anchorites of the mountains and forests of eastern Gaul, where our evidence is detailed and contemporary, as in the example of St. Martin. It is a new

[1] *Irish Monasticism* (Dublin, 1931), p. 260.

and somewhat alien element in the Roman Church of
the West, and we have seen that Celestine, the head of
the Roman Church in the early fifth century, regarded
it with no great favour. Its affinities are surely with
the solitaries and the little communities of the *lavrae* of
Egypt, Syria, Palestine, and Mesopotamia.

The Anchorites are often identified with the Culdees,[1]
with whom they had much in common; but the exact
nature of the Culdees is still undetermined. The name
appears to mean 'companion'[2] or 'dependent of God',
and the earliest occurrence of the name is in the Irish
glosses on the Psalms attributed to Columbanus of
Bobbio, where *Céli Dé* glosses a phrase which seems to
be equivalent to *vir Dei*.[3] As an organized body the
Culdees seem to have varied from one locality to another
and to have been at times a body within the monastic
bounds, yet forming an independent community within
the older and larger organization, as at Armagh; at
others, as at Ros-cré, a distinct body outside the community, yet living in close touch with it; at others again
constituting the entire community, as at Tallaght.[4] In
the monastic rule variously described as the *Rule of
Fothad na Canóine* (d. 819) of Donegal, or the *Rule of
Mo-Chuta*[5] (cf. p. 54 above), the duties of the *Céli Dé*
are classed by themselves, along with those of bishop,
priest, abbot, confessor, monk, and king. Kenney
believed that the term had a general sense of long
standing, but that as a distinct institution the Culdees

[1] The chief work of reference is still that of W. Reeves, *The Culdees
of the British Islands* (Dublin, 1864); but a new work on modern critical
lines is much needed.   [2] Cf. Lat. *comes*.
[3] Zimmer, *The Celtic Church* (ed. cit.), p. 100.
[4] Kenney, op. cit., p. 470.
[5] Its language is that of the early ninth century.

originated in what he regarded as the 'reform' movement of the eighth century, and that as a technical term
with a special spiritual association it dated from the
late ninth century. In Scotland the Culdees are not
known till later times. We find them established on St.
Serf's Island in Loch Leven by Macbeth. Is it possible
that the term 'servant of God' may have become general
as a result of various *cána* ('enactments') such as that of
Fothad na Canóine, which exempted them from any sort
of military service, save that of 'servants of God'?[1]

It is interesting to look ahead for a moment to the
later development of the Irish Anchorites. In the eighth
century, when the development had become more
systematized, and when also our documents give us
much fuller information, the Anchorites have developed
into an organized body, and this has no doubt given
rise to the idea that they originated in a reform movement at this period. These later Anchorites include
some important leaders, and during this period other
monasteries arose especially associated with the movement. The monasteries of Tallaght and Finglas, to the
north and south of the Liffey, as already mentioned
(p. 76), were known as the 'Two Eyes of Ireland', and
Terryglas on the Shannon in particular seems to have
been in some kind of obedience to Tallaght.

At the time when this monastery first comes before
us its head, and apparently its founder, was Máelrúain
(d. 792), perhaps the most important of the Anchorites
at this time. He was the 'tutor' (*aite*) of Oengus 'the
Culdee', the most famous literary man of the movement.

[1] It is perhaps worth noting that the Theodosian Code (A.D. 368)
forbade monks to escape taxes by going to the desert.

His origin, or at least some family connexion, was in
Munster, and he seems to have elevated the community
as a centre of Anchorite discipline, from which his
pupils, i.e. certain saints who had studied under him at
Tallaght, carried his teaching to their own monasteries.
The names of these saints and their centres are enumerated in a brief text contained in the *Book of Leinster*,
written in the twelfth century at Terryglas in the north
of Tipperary. The text bears the title: 'The Folk of the
Unity of Tallaght, i.e. after Patrick and after the twelve
apostles of Ireland'. Then follows a list of twelve saints,
headed by Máelrúain of Tallaght, and their distribution assigns three to Tallaght, five to Tipperary, two to
Cork, one each to Westmeath and Clare. Flower notes
that a versification of the names which follows, attributed to Cormac mac Cuilennáin, suggests that the
tradition came to Terryglas by way of Cashel—that in
fact, it is derived from Munster.[1] The text is interesting
also as a general indication of the 'unity' of a Mother
House.

Tallaght seems to have been outstanding for its ascetic
discipline. The literary works to which it gave birth and
a number of anecdotes show its Abbot Máelrúain as a
grave and relentless disciplinarian. A charming story is
told of him in the so-called *Rule of Tallaght*, cap. 50.
Máelrúain, we are told,

did not approve of listening to music. There was an anchorite of Desert Laigen who used to play the pipes. . . . His
name was Cornán (? 'the little horn-pipe player'), one upon
whom lay the grace of God. Máelrúain sent him a present
(doubtless a *eulogium*) to make fellowship with him in prayer
and supplication. Cornán said to Máelrúain's monks:

[1] Flower, 'The Two Eyes of Ireland', loc. cit. p. 70; cf. p. 71.

G

'I should like to play music for Máelrúain.'

On hearing this Máelrúain said:

'Tell Cornán that these ears of mine shall not be delighted with earthly music until they are delighted with the music of heaven.'[1]

The story illustrates very well the rigid ascetic ideals ascribed to the Anchorites of the eighth century.

Later tradition, however, here as in the East, often ascribes to these stern ascetics a pleasure and intimacy with wild things which is at once our envy and our despair. St. Moling, the Leinster saint (cf. p. 108 below) had as companions not only the fanatical Suibhne, but also a fox and a wren, and 'a little fly that used to buzz to him when he came from matins'.[2]

The Celtic Church is especially remarkable for two features. The first is the austere form of its discipline. The second is its intellectual activity, and especially its abundant flowering of a special class of poetry. I shall speak more fully of this literary development in the following lecture. Here I want to watch the hermits and contemplatives as they perfect themselves in their religious discipline, and to trace the witness to their life of the spirit on our maps and in the ruins of their little homes in solitary places.

In the East, in Egypt, Syria, and Palestine, the commonest form of austerity was the life of the religious devotee either in solitude in caves, or else in a *lavra*, a small community of monks still living in caves, though even in the fourth century buildings were erected in

[1] *Rule of Tallaght*, ed. E. Gwynn, *Hermathena*, xliv, 2nd suppl. vol. Dublin, 1927, p. 31.

[2] *The Birth and Life of St. Moling*, edited and translated by Whitley Stokes (London, 1907), p. 57.

some of these monastic settlements. Caves were a natural habitation of the Anchorite in that climate, but the more important monastic centres, like the monastery of St. Macarius in Egypt, and the monastery in Mount Sinai, soon had large buildings. In the *vitae* of the Syrian saints we hear frequently of 'pits' into which the saints used to retire for periods of retreat. St. Theodore of Sykeon (cf. p. 158 below) used to retire into an underground pit, especially during Lent. In Gaul extreme forms of austere penitential discipline seem to have had a relatively restricted influence, but here also a religious community or *monasterium* consisted of perhaps a group of cells, or of small chambers cut in the rock, or small wooden chambers. The picture which Sulpicius Severus gives us of the *turba monachorum* which constituted his little community in Aquitaine in the late fourth century is of just such a small unorganized collection. We have a contemporary picture also (cf. p. 47 above) of the Syrian monk Abraham and his hermitage, a hut thatched with reeds, and later of a small group of monks forming a community under his guidance, and ultimately the monastery of Cierges. Again Sulpicius Severus gives us a glimpse of this early severe austere penitential discipline in St. Martin's early community in the caves of Liguge at a time when the saint would still be under the influence of his former life as a solitary in the island retreat of Gallinaria; but he soon left this little *lavra*, as we may call it, for the *magnum monasterium*, Marmoutier.

In Britain the climate could hardly permit of the extensive cave development of the East, and it is not impossible that the word may have become a technical term in the theological diction in the West for a religious retreat, as *castra* was used in the specialized sense of a monastery. Gildas hurls at Maelgwn, the contemporary prince of Gwynedd, reproaches for this worldly life, reminding him that in youth he frequented the *speluncae*, 'caves', of the martyrs. Real caves, occupied by hermits, were certainly an institution in Britain, however.[1] Many late legends refer to the habit of early saints, including St. Ninian, of retiring into caves for periods of solitude,[2] and many caves exist which have Christian symbols among the *graffiti* on their walls.[3] In the Irish *Annals of the Four Masters* there is an interesting entry s.a. 898 of the obit of Caenchomhrac 'of the caves' (*na uaimh*) of Inishbófin. The word may here have a literal sense, for the numerous caves on the island have been used at all times as religious retreats and were occupied by priests hiding from Cromwell's soldiers. But the island was a monastic settlement from the time of St. Colmán (cf. p. 136 below).

The austere discipline of the Irish Church is written heavily across the place-names of our maps. The use of the word *desert, dysart* is an obvious link with the East, quite independent of Gaul. Its origin is clearly in the *deserta*, the original home of eremitism in Egypt and Syria and Palestine, and its use in Celtic lands is closely linked with this original connotation. We may instance *Dysert Décláin*, the principal sanctuary of the southern Dési (modern Decies) at Ardmore at the mouth of the

---

[1] Is it possible to see here an explanation of the 'earth-houses', commonly called 'caves' ('weems', Gael. *uaimh*) sometimes with a beehive cell attached, still underground, such as are common in some parts of Lowland Scotland, Cornwall, and Ireland? Cf. p. 148, n. 4 below.

[2] See A. P. Forbes, *Lives of S. Ninian and S. Kentigern* (Edinburgh, 1874), pp. 284 f.

[3] See Joseph Anderson, *Scotland in Early Christian Times*, 2nd series (Edinburgh, 1881), pp. 183 ff.

Blackwater on the Munster coast; Dysart in Westmeath,
the seat of Moeltuile mac Noechuire, evidently one of
Máelrúain's disciples, whose name appears first on the
list of twelve saints headed by Máelrúain of Tallaght, in
the little text of the 'Unity of Tallaght' referred to
above. In Fife we have the well-known *Dysart*; and
there are many other examples.

The word which most clearly demonstrates the close
connexion of our Celtic ascetics with the East is the
word *Marthyr*. A well-known example is Merthyr-Tydvil
in Glamorgan. Originally the word *martyrium* meant
simply 'witness', and the Christian sense of one who
suffers death is a gradual specialized development.
Already in the early centuries the word had come to be
used of a specialized form of Christian witness, with an
implication of renunciation of worldly pleasures, and in
this sense it was used by the early Fathers of the Church
of the early martyrdom of the ascetic life.[1] The Arabic
Life of Pachomius makes it clear that to him martyrdom
was consummated by an enforced continuation of life;
and in the *Apophthegmata*, believed to have been in circulation at least as early as the fourth century, a cell
occupied for many years by two young disciples of St.
Macarius is referred to by the saint after their death
as their *martyrion*. St. Basil declares that anyone can be
a martyr without persecution or scourges or fire, and
this specialized development of the term is enunciated
by Athanasius in *Doctrina ad Monachos*: 'The martyrs
were often consummated in a battle that lasted only
for a moment; but *the monastic institute obtains a
martyrdom* by means of a daily struggle. We are . . .

[1] E. E. Malone, 'The Monk and the Martyr', *Studia Anselmiana*,
xxxviii (1956), p. 201.

continuing the struggle until the last breath.'[1] It is clear that in such passages there is no implication of death.

It is in this last sense, tantamount to *ascesis*, that we may suspect that the word 'martyr' has left eastern traces, not only in our British place-names, but also in our Irish records. In the most archaic piece of Irish prose that we possess, the *Codex Canonum Hibernicorum Camaracensis*, generally referred to as the *Cambrai Homily*,[2] the text of which dates from the second half of the seventh century or the beginning of the eighth, three kinds of martyrdom are distinguished:

Now there are three kinds of martyrdom which are counted as a cross to man, that is to say, white martyrdom, and green (*glas*) martyrdom, and red martyrdom. This is the white martyrdom to man, when he separates for the sake of God from everything he loves, although he suffer fasting or labour thereat. This is the green (*glas*) martyrdom to him, when by means of them (fasting and labour) he separates from his desires, or suffers toil in penance and repentance. This is the red martyrdom to him, endurance of a cross or destruction for Christ's sake, as has happened to the apostles in the persecution of the wicked and in teaching the law of God. These three kinds of martyrdom are comprised in the carnal ones who resort to good repentance, who separate from their desires, who pour forth their blood in fasting and in labour for Christ's sake.[3]

[1] Ibid., p. 226. See, for the Greek text, Migne, P.G. xxviii, col. 1424.
[2] Text and translation by Stokes and Strachan, *Thesaurus Palaeohibernicus*, ii (Cambridge, 1903), pp. 244 ff.; cf. p. xxvi.
[3] In connexion with this passage the editors call attention to a very interesting note by Sir Richard Burton on a passage in *The Thousand Nights and a Night* (vi. 250), in which 'red death', 'green death', and 'black death' are distinguished; and Burton adds the following remark, apparently with reference to 'red death': 'Among the mystics it is the resistance of man to his passions.'

It will be noticed that in view of its early date the *Cambrai Homily* may be taken to represent the ascetic thought of the Anchorites. It should be added that the Old Irish so-called *Rule of Columcille*, to which reference was made above, probably of the ninth century in date, gives instructions to the recluse to bear 'a mind prepared for red martyrdom, a mind fortified and steadfast for white martyrdom'.

The most remarkable of all the institutions of the Celtic Church is the *Inis*, the island sanctuaries in which the more extreme of the ascetics lived. Scores of these fringe the coasts of the British Isles, and must ultimately be related to the island sanctuaries of the Italian and north Mediterranean coast of the fifth century. Here Rutilius Namatianus found monks to his great indignation in what he was pleased to describe as 'a shameful retreat'; and here on the island of Gallinaria St. Martin sojourned for a time on his way from Milan to Gaul. Here, just off the coast of Cannes, are the Lérins group, of which the monastery established by St. Honoratus *c.* 410 became almost at once virtually a little Christian university and the most distinguished intellectual centre in the western Mediterranean. Perhaps these island sanctuaries are a western development[1] satisfying the same need for seclusion as the cells of the desert solitaries in the East, and the forest hermitages of eastern Gaul and Brittany of the same period. We shall see that while in Ireland the forest sanctuaries have left no tangible trace, they are charmingly attested in the hermit poetry.

[1] A large number of early Christian sanctuaries are found also on the islands and peninsulas of Brittany. See J. Chagnolleau, *Les Îles de l'Armor* (Paris, 1951), *passim.*

The island sanctuaries of Britain[1] are not peculiar to
any one area or country, though by far the larger number are found off the coast of Ireland. Perhaps the most
famous in Britain are Iona and Lindisfarne because they
are the homes of St. Columba and St. Aidan and so are
well known to us from the Latin works of Adamnán and
Bede; but the account of the hermit Elgar in the opening section of the Book of Llan Dâv speaks of Bardsey
Island off the tip of the Caernarvonshire peninsula, the
terminus of a long pilgrims' route throughout the Middle
Ages, as the 'isle of twenty thousand saints'. The Isle of
Man shows remains of about two hundred keeills (Lat.
cellae). More remarkable are the isolated islands off the
Scottish coast—St. Kilda, with Churches to Christ,
Columba, and Brendan; North Rona with its oratory
and little graveyard, 'a mere rock in the wide ocean',[2]
sixty miles north of the Butt of Lewis; and the little
island of Sula-Skerry, ten miles west by south of Rona,
hardly a third of a mile in extent, herbless and at times
under wave-wash.[3] Yet here is a little chapel and beehive huts, and though the huts are kept in repair by
gannet-fowlers, the chapel is of the ancient type. How
did these hermits live? Graveyards on many of the islands
suggest permanent habitation.

The most spectacular and best-preserved of all these
island sanctuaries is the well-known settlement of bee-
nive cells near the summit of Sceilg Mhichíl, more frequently known as Skellig Michael, eight miles off the
western peninsula of Co. Kerry, and on a sheer rock.

[1] For a wide survey and study of the island sanctuaries the reader
may hope to consult the forthcoming book by Elizabeth Britton.

[2] Joseph Anderson, *Scotland in Early Christian Times* (Edinburgh, 1881),
p. 116.

[3] Ibid., p. 114.

The monastic settlement is seven hundred feet above the Atlantic, close to the edge of the cliff, and approached by a narrow path on the cliff edge and a series of steps cut in the rock. Here we find a group of five *clochán*, or 'bee-hive' cells, one larger building, and two rectangular structures, all of dry masonry, and protected from the precipice on the seaward side by a cashel wall, while near the cells are two cemeteries with a number of pillar stones cross-shaped and engraved.[1] As Joseph Anderson remarks, 'No wilder or more inaccessible situation can well be conceived.'[2] Only less remarkable are Inishmurray off the Sligo coast,[3] with the foundations of its monastic settlement almost perfectly preserved, including many of the beehive huts and several small stone churches, and the massive enclosing wall or cashel. The monastery of Nendrum in Strangford Loch off the coast of Co. Down in the east has been fully excavated,[4] thus enabling us to trace in detail the life of an early monastic community, as distinct from a retreat of hermits.[5] One of its clochán, believed to have been a workshop, contained small

[1] For some excellent views of the Sceilg Michíl monastery, see A. Mahr, *Christian Art in Ancient Ireland* (Dublin, 1932), vol. i, plates 2–4; and more recently, see the fine series of plates in Mlle F. Henry's article referred to in note 5, below. Also L. de Paor, 'A Survey of Sceilg Mhichíl', *Journal of the Royal Society of Antiquaries of Ireland*, lxxxv (1955), pp. 174 ff.

[2] Op. cit., p. 81.

[3] See H. G. Leask, *Irish Churches and Monastic Buildings*, i (Dundalk, 1955), p. 13.

[4] See the account by R. C. Lawlor, *The Monastery of Saint Mochasi of Nendrum* (Belfast, 1925).

[5] For a recent valuable discussion of ecclesiastical and other structures of our period in Co. Kerry and elsewhere, see F. Henry, 'Early Monasteries, Beehive Huts, &c.', *Proceedings of the Royal Irish Academy*, vol. 58, section C, no. 3 (1957), pp. 45 ff.

crucibles with the remains of enamel, pincers and tools for handling them, and small pieces of slate on which were scratched fragments of Celtic design—evidently trial pieces.[1]

The architectural features of these early monastic and anchoritic settlements are in general fairly uniform and characteristic. There are usually one or more tiny beehive cells, commonly without any opening except a door, though there is sometimes also a tiny unglazed window, perhaps only for ventilation. Generally there is also a chapel, about twelve feet long[2] more or less, with a simple stone altar, and one or two ambries. The chapel is generally rectangular internally, but rounded externally at the corners, (e.g. Teampull Sula-Sgeir) with an internal batter of corbelling towards the roof (e.g. Teampull Ronán).

All early Irish stone buildings are extremely small.[3] There are no large churches, but instead we find groups of small churches close together as in early Armenia. Perhaps the largest, though not an early, group of churches is at Glendalough in the Wicklow Hills in eastern Ireland. But the simplicity of the architecture may easily deceive us. The building technique is sometimes surprisingly impressive. The interior of the clochán or beehive' cells excavated by Françoise Henry on the island of Inishkea North in Clew Bay off the coast of Co. Mayo shows careful corbelling,[4] and the beehive cells

---

[1] These precious mementos of the activities of the monks are on view in Belfast Municipal Museum.

[2] Cf. St. Benignus on Aran Mór across Galway Bay.

[3] Cf. Leask, op. cit., passim.

[4] Excellent photographs of the interiors of two of these little cells were taken by T. H. Mason, and published by F. Henry in the *Journal of the Royal Society of Antiquaries of Ireland*, 1945, pp. 127 ff.

on Skellig Michael are a masterpiece of building construction with simple materials.[1]

The most perfect survival of a number of single oratories, built corbel fashion on a rectangular plan, that of the Gallerus Oratory in Co. Kerry,[2] is surprisingly competent in technique, while architecturally unpretentious. It is built of selected stones, partly tooled and fitted together carefully with no mortar used structurally, though with some fine mortar used as filling internally, a kind of internal pointing, while pick and punch have given a smooth face to the interior faces of the stones. Internally there is a roughly pointed vault, while externally the walls are curved, somewhat like a boat, and there is a west door and a small east window, its rounded head scooped out of two stones, with the effect of an internal splay. But the most striking feature of this little masterpiece is that, as in the building of the *clocháns*, the stonework is so laid at a slight angle as to direct the rain outwards from the fabric, so that, although near the rainy Kerry coast, the building has always remained bone-dry inside.

We do not know the date of these structures; island sanctuaries had sprung up and were a recognized institution round the British Isles by the sixth century at latest, as is clear from the choice of Iona by St. Columba; and that his choice was a deliberate one is shown by the selection of Lindisfarne by his representatives, and by that of Inishbófin off the coast of Co. Mayo in the west of Ireland by St. Colmán when, after the Synod of Whitby in 663, he repaired with his followers, going

---

[1] See especially A. Mahr, op. cit., plate 4; and F. Henry's plates, loc. cit.

[2] Leask, op. cit., pp. 21 ff.

first to Iona, and then to Inishbófin. But already in 617 St. Donnan, a contemporary of St. Columba, had been massacred with all his followers while celebrating mass on the island of Eigg in the Inner Hebrides.[1] Did St. Columba choose Iona because such island sanctuaries were already an established institution? Or did he in- augurate a new fashion in the Celtic Church? It was evidently already widespread in the Celtic Church in the sixth century. It is stated by Adamnán[2] that one of Cormac's three voyages undertaken to seek a *deserta* in the northern ocean failed because he had taken with him a certain monk who had not obtained the per- mission of his abbot. Evidently the mass movement to the islands was already in full swing, and this passage from Adamnán possibly suggests that it was at times a source of monastic disagreement.

The movement evidently reached its height in the seventh and eighth centuries. The Brough of Birsay in Orkney is believed to be a Celtic settlement of the seventh century. Dicuil,[3] a monk who seems to have been living on Iona under Abbot Suibhne (d. 772) and who was familiar with the Court of Charlemagne in 814 and still alive in 825, speaks of *Thile* (i.e. *Thule*, Iceland), of which he had received an account from certain religious who had lived there from February to August in 795. He also tells of anchorites who had occupied the islands round Britain and Ireland and the Faroes for nearly a century, but who were now driven

[1] Cf. the *Annals of Ulster*, and other Irish annals, and also the *Calendar of Oengus*. For a general collection of the evidence, see W. Reeves's edition of *Adamnán's Life of St. Columba* (Dublin, 1857), pp. 303 ff.

[2] Book I, cap. 6.

[3] For the important evidence of Dicuil, see Kenney, op. cit., pp. 545 ff., and the references there cited.

out by Vikings. We learn from Adamnán[1] that Brude, the king of the Northern Picts, converted by St. Columba, commanded his *subregulus* in the Orkneys to give protection, by Columba's request, to Cormac úa Liatháin when he was driven from his course in the Northern Ocean on the second of his voyages referred to above. It would seem probable that the immunity which the islands seem—with the exception of Eigg— to have enjoyed during the sixth and seventh centuries came to an end in the Viking Age.

A word may be added on the history of Skellig Michael. Apart from some legendary references and others of doubtful historical value[2] we have a reference to 'Suibni of the Scelig' in the *Martyrology of Tallaght*, dating from the end of the eighth century,[3] as well as in the later martyrologies.[4] In the *Annals of Ulster* and the *Annals of Inisfallen* we learn that in 824 Étgal of Skellig was carried off by the heathen (i.e. Vikings),[5] and died of hunger and thirst. In 882 the *Annals of Inisfallen* record the death of Flann, son of Cellach, abbot of Skellig, and the settlement evidently went on, for the *Annals of the Four Masters* mention the death of Blathmhac of Skellig in 950, while in 1044 the same Annals record the death of Aodh of Skellig Michael, referred to in the *Inisfallen Annals* as 'the noble priest, the celibate, and the chief of the Gaedhil in piety'. We have no further reference in the annals, but towards the close of the Middle Ages a chapel was added to the earlier group, and the older buildings were kept in repair. Indeed,

[1] *Life of St. Columba*, Book II, cap. 42.
[2] For the most recent and valuable account of Skellig Michael, including its history, see F. Henry, 'Early Monasteries, &c.' (ed. cit.), p. 115.
[3] Compare p. 143, note 3 below.
[4] See F. Henry, loc. cit., n. 4.
[5] For other and fuller references to this event, see F. Henry, loc. cit.

many of the island sanctuaries throughout Celtic lands
continued in use as sanctuaries, and doubtless as places
of pilgrimage, throughout the Middle Ages, as is clear
from the numerous ruins of medieval churches.

There can be no doubt that these island sanctuaries are closely connected with the peregrination and
penance which are among the most important developments of eremitism in the Early Celtic Church. We
have already seen the value placed on voluntary exile
in eremitical literature. Exile was also often prescribed as a punishment for the greater offences, especially homicide. Indeed, the Scilly Isles had already
been used as a penal settlement in the Roman period,
and after the condemnation of the Priscillianists some
of their members were banished to the Scillies. In
Ireland the exile was sometimes banished to another
country, or it might be only to another abbot.[1] We
have references to *peregrinatio* definitely enjoined as
a penance, including the well-known story of St.
Molaisse or Laisrén, St. Columba's *anmchara* or confessor, who, according to one tradition, condemned him
to perpetual exile to undertake the conversion of as
many souls as had perished in the Battle of Culdremhne,
for which Molaisse held him responsible.[2] This penance, as J. T. McNeill points out,[3] apparently implies
that the old penalty for homicide was applied by
the Synod of Teltown, although Adamnán, our authority here, refers to their action as excommunica-

[1] See the interesting note by J. T. McNeill and H. M. Gamer,
Medieval Hand-books of Penance (New York, 1938), p. 34,.

[2] But this does not necessarily mean missionary work. It might refer
to mission work (e.g. among the 'apostate Picts'); but in any case the
reference is late.

[3] 'Exile in the Penitentials and in the Irish Church', *Revue celtique*, xl.334ff.

tion;[1] and McNeill compares the command of St. Ita to
St. Brendan, whose negligence has caused the death of
a youth by drowning, and who is ordered to become a
wanderer on the earth, teaching others and bringing souls
to Christ.[2] The *Brehon Laws* seem to recognize the authority of the *anmchara* to send penitents on pilgrimage.

In a discipline where eremitism and penance played
so large a part it is not surprising to find that as early
as the seventh century[3] a system of private penance had
already developed, though it is believed that it was
not instituted on the Continent till much later. In the
Celtic Church, as a part of this system of private penance, a monk living an eremetical life had as a companion sharing his cell his *anmchara*, or 'soul-friend'
(Welsh *periglour*) to whom he made his confession and
who prescribed his penance (cf. p. 149 f. below). The
system, which does not appear in the Roman Church
of the period, would seem to be a natural development
among the desert solitaries of the East, and may possibly
be related to the *syncellus*, 'one who shares a cell' in the
Greek Church. In the story of the exile imposed on St.
Columba by St. Molaisse, Molaisse is acting as Columba's
anmchara. The drawing up of *Penitentials*, codes of regu-
lated systems of penance for specified sins, was among
the literary activities of the Anchorites, as we shall see,
and the austerities imposed in these penitential systems
were often of great severity. Even if we discount some
items of these penances for reasons to be suggested
later, yet it must be freely admitted that the austerities
of the Celtic Church actually vouched for in historical

---

[1] Op. cit., Book III, cap. 3.
[2] *Vita Prima S. Brendani* (Plummer, *V.SS.Hib.* i. 141).
[3] Kenney, p. 238.

sources are extremely rigorous, and some of them come curiously close to those of the Syrian saints.

Bede tells us of a man 'of simplicity of mind and modest mien (*homo simplicis ingenii ac moderatae naturae*) who for severe bodily penance used to stand in the water of the Tweed at Old Melrose, with the river up to his neck, reciting the psalms and prayers. In winter, Bede assures us, he would stand in the frozen river with the broken ice swirling round him, while the wondering by-standers would say:

'Brother Drycthelm, it is wonderful how you can endure such bitter cold';

to which this master of understatement would reply:

'I have seen greater cold';

and when again they persisted:

'It is wonderful that you are willing to practise such austerity',

this true son of the Border would reply:

'I have seen greater austerity.'[1]

With this passage it is interesting to compare the austerity of St. Theodore of Sykeon who, on the night of the Feast of the Epiphany, went down from the chapel to a ford in the river with a number of the clergy and the laity, and alone entered the water, and

stood there until all the reading from the prophets, apostles and Gospels was over, as well as the rest of the liturgy; so that at the end of the service he could only with difficulty pull up his feet all covered with mud and icicles frozen on to them, and thus he re-entered the oratory with psalm singing.[2]

[1] Bede, *H.E.* v. 12.

[2] Dawes and Baynes, *Three Byzantine Saints*, p. 98. I am indebted to Mr. John McQueen, who pointed out to me the correspondence of these two passages.

In a note to this passage the editor reminds us that in the Greek Church the baptism of Christ in Jordan is commemorated on the day of the Epiphany, 6 January. It would seem possible that Drycthelm's austerity is a celebration of the same rite as that of St. Theodore. Palladius tells us in the *Lausiac History* (cap. 38) that on one occasion Evagrius as a penance stood naked all night long in a well so that his flesh was frozen.

A little anonymous ninth-century poem describes the way of life which the Anchorite strove to follow in 'a hidden secluded little hut', with 'a cold fearsome bed where one rests like a doomed man', his food 'dry bread weighed out, water from a bright and pleasant hill-side', an 'unpalatable meagre diet, diligent attention to reading, renunciation of fighting and visiting', 'withered emaciated cheeks, skin leathery and thin', and withal 'I should love to have Christ son of God visiting me, and that my mind should resort to Him.' But it is significant that the ascetic expects to follow his life of mortification in the neighbourhood of a community. 'Let the place which shelters me amid monastic enclosures be a delightful hermit's plot hallowed by religious stones, with me alone therein.'[1]

The most extreme form of asceticism known to me from early Ireland is associated with the word *geilt*. The word is usually translated by modern writers as 'lunatic' or 'madman'. This is largely due to the literary influence of a late saga about a certain Suibhne,[2] a king

---

[1] Text and translation by Gerard Murphy, *Early Irish Lyrics* (Oxford, 1956), no. 9.

[2] The story of the *Buile Suibhne* is edited and translated by J. G. O'Keefe (London, 1913). It is assigned in its present form to the latter part of the twelfth century. See G. Murphy, *Studies* (1931).

H

of the sixth century,[1] who is said to have become *geilt* as the result of a vision in the sky during the Battle of · Moyra, an historical battle fought in A.D. 637. From this time on Suibhne flees from human society, abandoning his kingdom, leading a wandering life alone with wild nature, growing feathers and flying, and even haunting the tree-tops like a bird,[2] and subsisting solely on a strictly vegetarian diet, cresses and brook-lime and such herbs as he could gather. He is, nevertheless, befriended by St. Moling, a Leinster saint (d. 697), and on his death Moling buries him in consecrated ground, and despite Suibhne's fantastic behaviour, the saga-teller adheres throughout to the tradition that it was not the result of true madness, but of a deliberate way of life. The word *geilt* itself, and many of the most fantastic features of Suibhne, including the vision in the sky in battle, are all found in early Norse literature—where those who look up in battle are said to become *geilt*,[3] and close parallels occur also in medieval Welsh and ·Scottish literary and hagiographical tradition.

The story of Suibhne was evidently well known. A reference to his becoming *geilt* during the Battle of Moyra occurred also in an early Irish codex known

[1] The text refers to him as a king of the Dál nAraide in Co. Down; but Dalriada in northern Ireland or Scotland is more probable. See K. H. Jackson, 'The Motive of the Three-fold Death in the story of Suibhne Geilt', in *Essays and Studies presented to Professor Eóin MacNéill* (Dublin, 1940), p. 540.

[2] Among many passages reference may be made to cap. 59 and to the poem in cap. 61 in which Suibhne refers to himself as spending the night in various trees.

[3] Cf. D. E. Martin Clarke, *Hávamál* (Cambridge, 1923), str. 129 and note. Cf. also the Norwegian *Kongs Skuggsjo* ('*King's Mirror*') translated, with notes, by Kuno Meyer, 'The Irish Mirabilia in the Norse "Speculum Regale"', *Ériu* iv (1908), pp. 1 ff.   [4] Cf. Jackson, loc. cit.

as the *Book of Aicill*,[1] and his saga tells us that there
were many other men in Ireland who, like Suibhne,
lived ascetic lives as hermits or recluses, and who are
similarly *geilt*. We have indeed two other full-scale
sagas in which *gealta* (sing. *geilt*) are prominent, and
many other early references, all of which bear witness to
a widespread tradition of warriors who flee from battle
and become *geilt*, or 'volatiles' owing to their horror of
the slaughter.[2] The connexion with battle and the subsequent withdrawal and anchorite's life recall one of
the stories told to account for St. Columba's withdrawal
from Ireland after the Battle of Culdremhne, in atone-
ment for the number of the slain (cf. p. 102 above).
Both Columba and Suibhne were of royal blood, and so
have been regarded as having special responsibilities
for the battles. The story of Suibhne and the Welsh
and Scottish parallels all point to the sixth and seventh
centuries as the period in which the cycle originated.

The reference in the *Book of Aicill* also tells us that
Suibhne left many stories and poems behind him, and
many poems ascribed to him in later times are chiefly
concerned with his relations with wild nature. These
echo the traditional earlier poetry ascribed to him, for in
a codex dating from the eighth or ninth century, preserved in the monastery of St. Paul in Carinthia, five
poems have been preserved, some of which are believed
to be of earlier date than the codex itself,[3] and one of

[1] This ancient codex once preserved a law tract called *Bretha Étgid*
which was transcribed into later manuscripts. See D. Binchy, *Proceedings of the British Academy*, XXIX (1943), p. 28. The text is published
in the *Ancient Laws of Ireland*, III, 83 ff. (Dublin, 1865).

[2] Many famous saints had sprung from Roman military families,
e.g. Pachomius, St. John Chrysostom, St. Martin and his disciple
Victor, St. Januarius of Naples, St. Victricius of Rouen, and many others.

[3] For text, translation, and comment, see W. Stokes and J. Strachan,
Thesaurus Palaeohibernicus, ii. 294. Cf. pp. xxxii f.

these (no. 3) is assigned by its heading to 'Suibhne Geilt'. It is a brief poem in praise of Suibhne's little oratory, ivy-clad apparently:

My little oratory in Tuaim Inbir is not a full house . . .
With its stars last night, with its sun, with its moon. . . .
God from Heaven, He is the thatcher who hath thatched
it. . . .
A house wherein wet rain pours not,
A place wherein thou fearest not spear-points,
Bright as though in a garden, and it without a fence
around it.

It is clear that Suibhne is a recluse, and his oratory is the woodland. Next to this poem is another in the same manuscript, a devout little poem assigned by its heading to St. Moling, Suibhne's friend and protector, which the editors think may well have been composed by the saint himself. Elsewhere also Moling has celebrated his friendship for Suibhne.[1]

These early poems, and the nature of the story, suggest[2] that in the original tradition Suibhne was a fanatical recluse, and St. Moling his anmchara, or 'confessor'. Both are practising the eremetical life, Suibhne's reflecting an extreme kind which soon passed out of practice everywhere and was perhaps never firmly established in the West. In the following centuries we shall find much poetry ascribed to anchorites[3] closely similar in

[1] See W. Stokes, *Anecdota from Irish Manuscripts*, ii (Halle a. S., 1908), 20 ff., 24, 27.
[2] For a fuller study of the subject I may refer to my article on 'Geilt' in *Scottish Gaelic Studies*, v (1942), pp. 106 ff.
[3] Perhaps the most sustained poetical composition on the subject is the anonymous ninth-century poem commonly referred to as *King and Hermit*, translated by Kuno Meyer, op. cit., p. 47. See also Gerard Murphy, op. cit., no. 8.

tone to that of Suibhne and Moling in the early codex. Extreme asceticism, such as that of Suibhne and the 'many *gealta*' in Ireland in his day, soon became transformed by the laughing Irish shanachie into rollicking satire. But the word itself is significant. The root occurs frequently in early Irish literature and glosses,[1] and is believed to be derived from the root *gel-*, 'to pasture', 'graze', and no doubt has reference to the diet of herbs and cresses of Suibhne and the other anchorites in our early poems.

A close analogy to these *gealta* of the Irish Christian Church, who shun the society of men and live alone with wild nature under the open heavens or even in the trees, is found in the recluses of the Syrian desert, referred to by Greek writers as βοσκοί 'Grazers' and δενδρῖται 'Tree-dwellers'. The βοσκοί are so described,[2]

because they had no houses, ate neither bread nor meat, and drank no wine; but dwelt constantly on the mountains, and passed their time in praising God by prayers and hymns. ... At the usual hour of meals they each took a sickle and went to the mountain to cut some grass as though they were flocks in pasture; and this served for their repast.

[1] Whitley Stokes collected and discussed some of these references in *Goidelica* (2nd edition, London, 1872), p. 60.

[2] Sozomen, *Hist. Eccles.* vi. 33. 2. They flourished from the fourth century. This Greek word βοσκός, lit. 'a herdsman', 'one who feeds', is used in patristic writings in the sense of a 'grazer', one who lives on grass like cattle and avoids human company. Cf. further Cyril of Skythopolis, *Vita Sabae* (ed. Schwarz, p. 99, l. 19), where it is used with reference to those who joined Sabas in founding his *lavra* in A.D. 483; also Evagrius, *H.E.* i. 21 (*P.L.* xxxvi, col. 2480; also ed. Bidez and Parmentier, p. 30, l. 24; νέμονται δὲ τὴν γῆν βοσκοὺς καλοῦσι, Leontius of Cyprus, *Vita S. Symeonis*, cap. iv, *P.G.* xciii, col. 1688; cf. further H. Leclercq, in Cabrol and Leclercq, *Dictionnaire*, s.v. *Monachisme*, col. 1829. Cf. also Theodoret, *Philotheos*; Migne, *P.L.* lxxii, 1490.

The extreme asceticism symbolized by the *gealta* of many of our Irish sagas and poems is associated in these sources with battles of the early historical period. It is not confined to Ireland, but can be traced in the earliest British (Welsh) versions of the Merlin legend, and it is known to have reached Scandinavia in the form of a *mirabile*. In the twelfth-century Latin composition, the *Speculum Regale* referred to above (p. 106), the majority of the *mirabilia* are drawn from Celtic sources and associated with the legends of the saints, of whom it is said that no other island of the size of Ireland contained an equally large number. A valuable section is devoted to the Culdees. It is significant that the passage relating specifically to *geilt* accurs in this Celtic hagiological context.

In connexion with Suibhne reference has also been made to the δενδρῖται or 'tree-dwellers',[1] a small number of ascetics related to the pillar-saints. John Moschus speaks of a monk Adolas who came from Mesopotamia and dwelt in a large plane tree and made a window through which he used to talk to visitors.[2] Among the *Opuscula* of the Maronites is the story of a saint who lived in a cypress tree in Syria.[3] In Europe we hear of Luke the 'pillar-saint', a monk of St. Zacharias on Mount Olympus, who had formerly used the hollow or perhaps the bole of a tree as a cell before graduating to his column.[3] Suibhne Geilt is at no very distant remove from the Syrian 'grazers' and 'tree-saints', whether we suppose that the more severe forms of penitential discipline of the Celtic Anchorites received a direct

---

[1] See Leclercq, *Dictionnaire*, s.v. *Dendrites*, and the references there cited.

[2] J. Moschus, *Pratum Spirituale*, P.G. lxxxvii, col. 2924.

[3] H. Delehaye, Bollandiste, *Les Saints Stylites* (Brussels and Paris, 1923), ch. V; compare Leclercq, loc. cit.

impetus from Syria, or whether, as is perhaps more probable, stories of these more extreme forms of Eastern asceticism have made their way to western Europe and formed the nucleus of the story of Suibhne's fanatical austerities. If the basis is merely literary, stories of these Eastern ascetics must have been in circulation in Ireland at an early date, probably not later than the eighth or ninth century. Yet he is connected with St. Moling in Irish tradition.

If we are right in believing that knowledge of the Eastern form of the ascetic life reached Ireland in the Age of the Saints, the question arises as to where it first took root on Irish soil and what is its chief centre of distribution. The explanation most frequently offered is that it was brought to Ireland by strangers coming from the East; or by Irishmen returning from foreign pilgrimage; or through literary channels. There is some slight evidence for all these views, but our difficulty is that we are almost totally without direct contemporary Irish records for this early phase. We have seen, however, that our indirect evidence suggests that literary material was coming into Ireland at this time from the Mediterranean countries, perhaps North Africa and Spain more especially. We have seen also that at this period Munster was in close touch with the intellectual life of these countries.

At the mouth of the River Blackwater in Munster on which Lismore stands is the island of Dair-inis, now identified on the strength of a colophon clumsily copied by a Breton scribe as the monastery where the *Collectio Canonum Hibernensis* was drawn up by 'Rubin of Dair-Inis and Cú-Chuimne of Iona'.[1] This is among the

[1] Kenney, op. cit., p. 248, and n. 273.

earliest literary works of the Irish Church, and the Breton colophon associating it with Dair-Inis is strong evidence that Dair-Inis no less than Lismore was in close contact with the Continent at this time. Brittany seems, in fact, to have been perhaps the chief route by which this text entered the country, where its importance quickly spread.[1] The monastery of Lismore on the River Blackwater and the important confederation of Munster monasteries of which it was the leader were in close touch with western Mediterranean culture.

Lismore was a monastic school of exceptionally high standard. In a brilliant study of the *De Mirabilibus* referred to above (p. 53), commonly known as the Pseudo-Augustine but long known to be an Irish composition, Père Grosjean has been able to show that the author was almost certainly a monk of Lismore. It is dedicated to 'the venerable bishops and priests of cities and monasteries, especially (*maxime*) *Carthaginensium*', and Grosjean has pointed out[2] that the reference is not to Carthage in North Africa, but to the monastic communities of St. Carthage (or St. Mochuda) of Lismore, the important monastery of the Dési (modern Decies) on the River Blackwater, founded, according to the Annals, in 636. The work is anonymous, but the author refers to a number of authorities, five of whom are Irishmen, the chief being a certain Eusebius to whom the author dedicates his epistle. All appear to be identical with Irish ecclesiastics of the seventh century known to us from other sources, notably from an unedited commentary

---

[1] Kenney, op. cit., p. 248, and the references there cited.
[2] 'Sur quelques exégètes irlandais', *Sacris Erudiri*, vii (1955), pp. 67 ff. Cf. also Kenney, op. cit., pp. 275 ff.

on the Seven Catholic Epistles at Carlsruhe. It is clear that Lismore was an active centre of Latin studies at this period, carrying on a measure of intellectual and literary correspondence both with other Irish religious houses and also with the Continent. The author of the *Pseudo-Augustine*, with his references to Carthage and Eusebius, was evidently a partaker in the literary trifling in vogue in Gaul and perhaps also in north-western Spain at this period (cf. pp. 54 f. above) and later, by which the names of great authors were assumed as a kind of nom-de-plume without the slightest intention to deceive.

To this area and milieu we may probably assign, at least in origin and nucleus, one if not two litanies of Irish saints edited by the late Charles Plummer.[1] The first of these, the *Litany of the Pilgrim Saints*, has been recently studied afresh by Dr. Kathleen Hughes,[2] who assigns it to the eighth or very early ninth century and who has shown that it was probably composed at the monastery of Lismore, on the River Blackwater in south Munster, founded, according to the Irish annals, in 636. The emphasis of the document is definitely on the south, with its pilgrim saints located on the coast, on the estuaries and islands—typically ascetic sites—though the outlook is not confined to Ireland. The fact pointed out by Plummer, however, that the saints are invoked from practically every county in Ireland, probably suggests, as I venture to think, that rather than a pocket litany for a private devotee, it was a textbook for general

---

[1] *Irish Litanies* (London, 1925), pp. 55–75. For the place of Irish litanies in the history of the Roman liturgical literature, see Cabrol and Leclercq, *Dictionnaire d'archéologie chrétienne et de liturgie*, s.v., cols. 1554 ff., and the references there cited.

[2] 'An Irish Litany of Irish Saints compiled *c.* 800', *Analecta Bollandiana*. lxxvii (1959).

reference, compiled by a monastic scholar with a generous reference bookshelf at hand, such as the libraries of
the bigger monasteries would have at this date. I should
be inclined to attribute its allusions[1] to Armenia, and
'Romans' (ind Romanaig)[2] and Egyptian monks, as well
as Britons, Saxons, and *Gaill* (? Gauls), to such literary
sources rather than to visitors to Ireland from these
countries.[3] The author knew his atlas. He was no be-
nighted provincial.

In these literary studies we are at the heart of the anchorite world. Lismore, on the upper bend of the Blackwater, and Ardmore, St. Déclán's monastery near its
mouth, were the two principal monasteries of the Dési
(Decies) in South Munster, and Lismore was perhaps
the most intellectual of the Munster monasteries.[4] It
was evidently famous for the performance of the Litany,
for in the *Triads of Ireland*,[5] attributed to the ninth
century, Lismore is mentioned in a list of the great
monasteries of Ireland as *Litanácht Hérenn Less Mor*,
'Lismore of the Litany' which calls to mind the developments of the Eastern Church. Moreover, the early
abbots of Lismore were well-known monastic leaders,
famous for their asceticism. St. Mochuda, formerly

---

[1] Cf. also *Sanas Cormaic*, edited by Kuno Meyer, *Anecdota from Irish Manuscripts*, iv (Halle a. S., 1912), p. 63.

[2] *Romani* generally refers to the reforming 'Roman' party in Ireland. See W. Ullmann, 'On the use of the term "Romani" in the sources of the Earlier Middle Ages', *Studia Patristica*, ii (1957), pp. 155-63.

[3] Reference should perhaps be made here, however, to the interesting point of similarity to a feature of Armenian architecture in the human heads forming the capitals of columns in the church at Rahan in Co. Offaly. See H. G. Leask, op. cit., pp. 88 f.

[4] Kenney, op. cit., pp. 451, 469.

[5] Edited by K. Meyer, Royal Irish Academy, Todd Lecture Series, xiii (1906).

abbot of Rahan, believed to have been expelled for his support of the Roman Easter, is among the early names of the *peregrini* of the 'pilgrim saints' (nos. 5 and 6), and others commemorated there are well known for their connexions with the Lismore circle.[1]

It would seem probable that Lismore was one of the southern centres of learning and continental contacts which stimulated the great ascetic communities of North Munster and Leinster, especially the little group of Clonferta-Molua, Mendrochet, and Ros-cré, and Clonenagh, with Cell-achid a little to the north and Terryglas to the west. Fintan of Clonenagh is renowned for the extreme asceticism of his rule—'The monks of Fintan, . . . who ate nothing but the herbs of the earth and water'[2]—and he is described in a list of saints in the Book of Leinster[3] as *caput monachorum totius Hiberniae.* He is closely associated with Máeldub, trained by the extremely ascetic St. Fechin, and in the *Martyrology of Oengus*[4] Máeldub is said to have possessed nothing in the world except his cloak and linen sheet, and never to have laid his head on a pillow. These and others who might be cited differ in nothing essential from the Syrian βοσκοί, or their own fellow countryman Suibhne Geilt.

The first Preface to the *Martyrology of Oengus* states that Oengus the Culdee was a member of the community of Fintan of Clonenagh and that it was in Clonenagh that he composed the greater part of this work, but that he completed it at Tallaght. We shall see

[1] Cf. Hughes, op. cit., p. 309.
[2] *Litany of the Saints of Ireland*, ed. cit., p. 61; cf. *Vita*, Plummer, *V.S.H.* ii. 4, 5, 7, 19, 22.
[3] Folio 370, cols. 3 and 4.
[4] Edited and translated by W. Stokes (London, 1905), pp. 224 f.

that the unity of Tallaght is the most intellectually outstanding group of houses associated with the so-called Anchorite Reform during the eighth century, and that Tallaght and Finglas across the Liffey took a leading part in the literary movement in the same period. It is safe to say that the most influential figure in the movement was Máelrúain himself. Little is known of his personal life. His name probably means 'the tonsured or devotee of Rúan', but if connected with Rúadán, which is less likely, it might associate him with modern Lorrha, one of the most important Munster houses, whose founder was said to be a member of the Eoganacht dynasty. He seems also, according to tradition, to have been a student of Fer-Dá-Crích, abbot of Dair-Inis (d. 747, *Annals of Ulster*).[1] His own early associations and training would seem the latest saint to be mentioned in the *Martyrology of Oengus*.

Our evidence on the whole suggests that the Age of the Saints probably began no later than the Age to which St. Patrick is assigned, but that whereas traditionally St. Patrick's influence was established earliest in the north, the monastic movement first entered the country from the south. We have also seen reason to think that whereas the Patrician Church passed directly from Britain to Ireland, perhaps under stimulus from the Church in Gaul, the monastic Church penetrated from Munster, where powerful monasteries were founded at an early date. This area, and in particular the monastery of Lismore and others on the Blackwater and the Barrow, were evidently in direct intellectual intercourse with the Continent in the sixth century,

[1] Kenney, op. cit., p. 469; cf. pp. 306, 352, n. 185.

especially with Aquitaine and most probably with Spain also. It is from these progressive Munster centres that the prominent anchorite foundations of the following period, notably Tallaght, Finglas, and Terryglas, drew their founders and their origin.

On the whole we may safely reject the distinction between the period and the institution of the Second and the Third Order of Saints. The distinction had no reality. It was created in the monastic scriptorium of a later age with the object of discrediting ascetic practice and eremitical separatism, in order to exalt the greater monastic houses and the Patrician Church. The so-called 'Third Order', who are to be identified with the Anchorites, belonged to the same monastic movement and the same period as the saintly founders of the large monasteries, with which they are very frequently, per-haps normally, closely associated.

In this relationship, as in the form of their ascetic discipline, they are closely comparable with the ascetics of the East, from whom Christianity in southern Ireland appears to have received a strong stimulus. By what precise channels and mediums this impetus was trans-mitted we can at present hardly confidently conjecture. Closer evidence is to be looked for from a comparative study of the earliest literary texts of the Irish and the Eastern Churches—a task which as yet few are quali-fied to undertake. In the meantime enough is known to show that the Anchorites are an integral part of the earliest Irish Church in the Age of the Saints—neither a later development nor a Reform. From the ruins of their lonely and austere settlements, and the peniten-tial nature of the place-names associated with them— *deserta, martyrion, spelunca (uaimh), insula (inis)*; from the whole-hearted admiration of their contemporary Bede, who was not a friend of their tenets; and most of all from their literature, to which we shall now turn, we must look upon the Anchorites as the fine flower of Irish spirituality in the Age of the Saints.

III

THE CELTIC CHURCH AND THE
ROMAN ORDER

In 597 St. Columba died and St. Augustine landed
in Canterbury. The coincidence is a dramatic one.
St. Columba, the greatest saint of the Celtic Church, is the
founder of the Order which had spread from Donegal
in Northern Ireland to Iona, and from there had established in Northumbria the form of Christianity which
we have been studying in the last lecture. It was virtually Irish Christianity of the sixth century, monastic
in organization, and to all intents and purposes independent and self-governing, though perfectly orthodox
in belief.

The clash between the two Churches was bound to
come. The form of Christian organization introduced
into Kent by St. Augustine was unlike that of the Celtic
Church. It made no claim to be either independent
or self-governing. It was in all matters directly under
obedience to Rome. But while the Celtic countries
shared to the full the orthodox views of the Church of
Rome, their remote position made them conservative.
They were failing to keep pace with modifications in the
Continental Church. To the Irish people and the members of the Columban Church in Britain a sudden
change in their church government, a modification in
their ecclesiastical system, involving a reduction of
monastic prestige, would have involved an economic

revolution. The Welsh, for their part, feared and disliked the suggestion of direct control from Rome through a bishop of Canterbury under a Saxon king. They were suspicious of the political implications. They liked their own ways, the traditions handed down to them by their own *'seniores'*.

Bede's *Ecclesiastical History* concentrates closely on this theme within the larger framework of the Conversion of Britain and the foundation of Christianity in our islands. Whether from lack of knowledge or from lack of interest, Bede says nothing of the Conversion of Wales or of Ireland to Christianity. He never mentions St. Patrick or Armagh, and dismisses in a sentence the statement (derived from Prosper) that Celestine sent Palladius as the first bishop to the Irish believing in Christ. He relegates the foundation of Whithorn to an aside. His concern with the Christianity of Ireland and of Scotland is limited to the Columban Church. His theme throughout is the Roman mission, first the two preliminary missions of St. Germanus (derived by Bede from the *Vita* of St. Germanus by Constantius) and then the real opening of his theme with the mission of St. Augustine from Pope Gregory to King Æthelberht of Kent and the foundation of the other English bishoprics, and the conversion of Northumbria. The conversion of the Northumbrian king Edwin he attributes—contrary to Celtic sources—to Bishop Paulinus of Canterbury. He moulds his narrative henceforth round the Paschal Controversy, and the gradual progress of the Celtic Church towards inclusion in the Roman Order. The consummation is reached towards the close of the *Ecclesiastical History* in the glowing panegyric and requiem on the English monk Ecgberht, who had, after long toil, brought the Columban Church into conformity with the Roman Order.

The British Church had been a source of uneasiness to the head of the Church in Rome for a long time. It had been the stronghold of the Pelagian heresy, and we have seen the anxiety with which Celestine, the bishop of Rome, viewed the speculative thought of Britain, and the care with which, through the missions of Palladius and of St. Germanus, he had 'sought to make the pagan island Christian and the Christian Island Catholic'. Now, a century and a half later, with the establishment of a powerful Teutonic kingdom in Kent under Æthelberht and his Frankish Christian wife Bertha, Pope Gregory realized that the moment had come for a fresh effort towards complete unity in the institutions of the western Church. To this end Bede relates[1] two distinct campaigns from Rome. The first had been made about the beginning of the seventh century under St. Augustine of Canterbury against the British Church in the west; the second was made in the time of Bishop Wilfrid at the Synod of Whitby in 663, when the issue turned on the dating of Easter (cf. p. 127 below), in which the Celtic usage had not adopted the practice of the Roman Church as fixed by Victorius of Aquitaine in 457.[2] The celebration of this, the greatest of all Christian festivals, on divergent dates by the adherents of the Celtic and the Roman orders in Britain was an obvious disadvantage, and a natural point on which the struggle for unity focused; but it must not be supposed

[1] *H.E.* ii. 2.
[2] For a recent article on the subject, see the Rev. Paul Grosjean, Bollandiste, 'Recherches sur les débuts de la controverse paschale chez les Celtes', *Analecta Bollandiana*, lxiv (1946).

that the struggle was at heart one of dry detail. Much deeper issues were at stake, as we shall see.[1]

The first of the two campaigns organized against the Celtic Church in Britain was undertaken by St. Augustine in person against the British. Bede is our sole authority for the facts. He relates this story as three distinct episodes in an elaborate ecclesiastical saga. And his account is given in pure oral narrative style, with all the conversations fully reported. It is a story full of picturesque details, with an elaborate setting and artificial framework. The style could hardly be a greater contrast to that of Bede's narrative when he is reporting transactions based on Canterbury documents. He must be following some saga original, which was divided into three episodes, consisting of two interviews between St. Augustine and a number of British bishops, followed after a short interval by their sequel in the Battle of Chester.

The first interview takes place on the borders of the West Saxons and the Hwicce at a place known as Augustine's Oak, perhaps at Aust, opposite Chepstow on the Severn. Augustine urges the British bishops to preserve Catholic unity *with him* (*secum*) and to join with him in undertaking the common labour of preaching the Gospel to the heathen (*gentibus*). The saint, in order to impress them, has recourse to a miracle—a measure for which Bede feels himself under the necessity of apologizing;[2] but the bishops say that they cannot abandon their former customs without the consent of

---

[1] On Victorius of Aquitaine and his tables, and the details of their dissemination and acceptance, see C. W. Jones, *Baedae Opera de Temporibus* (Cambridge, Mass., 1943), pp. 61 ff. See especially pp. 65 f.

[2] '*Justa necessitate compulsus*'.

their people and ask for a further and more representative conference. Accordingly a second conference is
arranged. Seven British bishops and a great many of
their most learned men (*plures viri doctissimi*) from the
monastery, as is made clear later, of Bangor on the Dee,
together with their abbot Dinoot, consult an Anchorite
'living among them',[1] who advises them to accept Augustine if he shows himself meek and lowly by rising to
greet them on their arrival—a typical Celtic touch.
Augustine, however, remains seated and accuses them
of acting in many ways contrary to the custom of the
Universal Church, and urges on them three things: to
keep Easter at the time prescribed; to administer baptism according to the Roman rite; *jointly with him* (*una
nobiscum*) to preach to the English. The British bishops
reply that they will do none of these things, nor accept
him as their archbishop, saying among themselves that
if Augustine would not rise to greet them then, how
much more would he hold them of little account if they
should subject themselves to him. Augustine replies
by a threat that if they will not accept peace with the
brethren[2] they must look to accepting war from their
enemies; and if they will not preach the way of life to
the nation of the English they shall suffer vengeance at
their hands.

Bede, we may be sure, is not himself responsible for
the actual form of the story. It is probably the composition of a strongly anti-Welsh Mercian monastery which
Bede has incorporated into his *History*, perhaps derived
more directly from Pecthelm of Whithorn, formerly

---

[1] 'Quendam virum sanctum ac prudentem qui apud eos anachore-
ticam ducere vitam solebat'.

[2] 'Si pacem cum fratribus accipere nollent'.

a monk of Malmesbury, from whom Bede tells us he obtained other Mercian stories.[1] But Bede shares to the full its anti-British (Welsh) bias. He goes straight on to relate that the prophecy of St. Augustine fell out just as he had threatened, and was fulfilled in the Battle of Chester, in which King Æthelfrith of Bernicia was victorious over the Welsh princes in 616.[2] Bede or his informant is selecting his material with a rigid intention to discredit the Welsh, whom he calls a *perfida gens*, and their army *nefandae militiae*. About the battle he only tells us that a large number of monks from the neighbouring monastery of *Bancornaburg*, presumably Bangor ys y Coed, Bangor-on-the-Dee, who had assembled near the site of the battle to pray for the combatants, were slaughtered by Æthelfrith owing to the cowardly flight of their leader, a certain Brocmail.

The fulfilment of Augustine's prophecy in the Battle of Chester forms the third episode and the climax of Bede's saga. He evidently possessed considerable information about the monastery of Bangor; and we know many details of the battle itself from Irish and Welsh sources. A comparison of these enables us to realize even more fully the bias of Bede's narrative and his evident bitterness against the Welsh. This is fully accounted for by the fact that whereas the Northumbrian Church had conformed to the Roman Order some nine or ten years before he was born, the Welsh apparently held aloof till long after his death.[3]

---

[1] e.g. *H.E.* v. 13, 18; cf. iv. 23.

[2] Not 613 as commonly stated in our history books. The Welsh annals are three years behind at this point.

[3] Ibid. v. 23; and also cf. Lloyd, *History of Wales*[2] (London, 1954), p. 203.

It has been observed recently[1] that despite Bede's
account the Easter question was probably never raised
at the conferences between St. Augustine and the
British bishops; but it is important to note that Bede
immediately adds as his own rubric that 'They did not
keep Easter at the correct date and did several things
which were against the unity of the Church.' Clearly to
Bede this was the crux of the whole matter, and his
final comment echoes the basic principle advanced by
all advocates of unity, 'They preferred their own traditions before all the Churches in the World, which in
Christ agree among themselves.'[2] It is the argument used
by Cummian, an abbot in southern Ireland in the letter
attributed to him, addressed to Segéne, abbot of Iona
c. 632–3, (cf. p. 130 below) in which he declares ironic-
ally: 'Roma errat; Jerusalem errat; Alexandria errat;
Antioch errat; totus mundus errat; solum tantum Scoti
et Britones rectum sapiunt',[3] and it echoes the rhetorical dogmatic statement of Vincent of Lérins two centuries earlier, that that is worthy of belief which has
been accepted *semper, ubique,* and *ab omnibus.*[4] We are
about to hear from Bede that Bishop Wilfrid of York
opened his speech at the Council of Whitby with the
same argument.[5]

The second campaign towards the unity of the Church
in Britain was directed later in the century towards the
north, where the Columban Order had prevailed in
the Northumbrian Church since the reign of Oswald. It

[1] M. Deanesly and the Rev. Paul Grosjean, Bollandiste, 'The
Canterbury Edition of the Answers of Pope Gregory I to St. Augustine',
Journal of Ecclesiastical History, x. 43.   [2] *H.E.* ii. 2.
[3] Haddan and Stubbs, *Councils,* ii, ii. 288; Migne, lxxxvii, col. 974.
[4] *Commonitorium,* cap. 4.   [5] Bede, *H.E.* iii. 25.

will be remembered that according to Bede's narrative St. Paulinus, having been sent by Pope Gregory in answer to St. Augustine's appeal for fellow workers, and having gone north as chaplain to Edwin's royal Kentish bride, had baptized Edwin[1] and his Northumbrian subjects in 627. Upon the death of Edwin and his son Osfrith in 632, however, Paulinus had been forced to flee for safety to Kent with the queen and her sons, and on the accession of Edwin's cousin Osric the country had reverted to paganism. Christianity was quickly restored on the accession of Aethelfrith's son Oswald.

Now, however, it was not the Roman Order of Christianity, introduced into Canterbury in 597 by St. Augustine, which became the Church of Northumbria, but the earlier form of the Celtic Church which had been introduced by St. Columba into Scotland, where Oswald had been converted to Christianity during his exile in the reign of Edwin. Oswiu, his brother and successor, had married a daughter of King Edwin, who naturally adhered to the Roman Order in which she had been instructed by Paulinus and to which she had continued to adhere during her exile in Kent, after Edwin's death.

A clash between the two Orders was bound to follow, and Bede focuses it picturesquely on the discrepancy in the date of Easter, the court and king celebrating it according to the old custom of the Celtic Church, while the queen with her chaplain and followers were still fasting and observing Palm Sunday. Perhaps the cleavage

---

[1] So also the Life of Pope Gregory the Great by the anonymous monk of Whitby. Nennius, writing c. 800, but using much earlier northern sources, claims that Edwin was baptized by Rhun map Urien (*Historia Brittonum*, cap. 63).

lay deeper, for Oswiu, a Gaelic speaker, favoured the
Celtic tradition in which he had been trained, whereas
his son Alchfrith, who had been trained under Wilfrid,
a zealous adherent of the Roman tradition, was already
taking active measures to promote Wilfrid[1] and rein-
state the Roman Order. The conflict between these two
loyalties culminated in the Council of Whitby in 663
with the triumph of the Roman party.

Accordingly a softer light is shed by Bede on his account of this debate than on that with the British bishops.
Again he presents us with a highly elaborate picture
of the contest, which took place in the presence of King
Oswiu, between Colmán, bishop and abbot of Lindisfarne, as spokesman for the Celtic Order, and Bishop
Wilfrid for the Roman. As the event took place only a
generation before Bede's own time we need not imagine
any elaborate written source, though the debate which
he professes to give us verbatim is necessarily an artificial report or reconstruction. In form it resembles the
debate before Edwin at York earlier in the century regarding the question of the introduction of Christianity.
In both debates a representative speaker of the two
opposing parties deploys, uninterrupted, his arguments
before the king, in the manner of forensic pleading
before a judge, and Bede's account is modelled on the
traditional procedure in a contest between rival rhetors
in a late Classical law court.[2]

At the close of the debate Óswiu gave his judgement

[1] *H.E.* iii. 25.
[2] The form evidently continued as a widespread literary convention.
It is apparently identical with one of the stories reported in Spanish
sources of the conversion of the Gothic king Reccared in Spain from
Arianism to the Catholic persuasion. See H. Bradley, *The Goths* (London,
1888), p. 328.

in favour of the acceptance of the Roman Order.[1] Colmán and many of his followers from Lindisfarne, both the Columban monks and even about thirty Saxons, were unwilling to accept the change. They departed to Iona and later to Inishbófin off the west coast of Mayo in Ireland. Bede's account of this little *navigatio* is our earliest narrative of a settlement of monks in the islands of the 'Blessed' in the western Ocean, of which we have many Irish stories. As Colmán and his party leave, Bede in a noble interlude pauses to picture for us the Celtic monks of the Church of Lindisfarne as it had been under Colmán and his predecessors, with their austere and idealistic way of life;[2] and he tells of the scholarship and generosity of the Irish monks among whom they had now gone.[3] Bede seems almost to be looking back nostalgically to the Celtic Church to which he still belonged in spirit. He had known and lived under King Aldfrith of Northumbria, who had been educated in the Irish tradition; and in his account of both Aidan and Colmán and of their way of life he gives us our most ideal picture of the Celtic Church as he had received it from the traditions of a generation before his own time.

Bede tells us[4] that when Laurentius succeeded Augustine in the bishopric of Canterbury he laboured indefatigably, not only on behalf of the new Church established among the English, but also in endeavouring to bring the Irish and the British Churches into conformity

---

[1] With Bede's account it is interesting to compare that of Eddius Stephanus, *Life of St. Wilfrid*, edited and translated by B. Colgrave (Cambridge, 1927), cap. x.
[2] *H.E.* iii. 26.   [3] Ibid. 27.   [4] Ibid. ii. 4.

with the Roman usage, especially in regard to the date
of Easter. Bede has preserved for us the text of a hor-
tatory epistle written by Laurentius and his fellow
bishops to the Irish bishops and abbots, praising the
reputation of both the Irish and the Britons, but
deprecating their separatism, on the grounds of information given him by Columbanus and Bishop Dagan
'coming to Britain'. Dagan had refused to eat with the
Saxon bishops, or even to stay in the same house. It is
a wise and tactful letter, making no reference to any
controversy, Easter or other, and it is in accordance
with its conciliatory tone that he mentions that he
has received his information from two of their own
bishops. Bede adds that Laurentius also wrote a letter
to the priests of the Britons urging them to enter with
him into Catholic unity, but his efforts met with no
success.

The south of Ireland, always in touch with continental
developments, accepted the Roman system of dating
for Easter almost thirty years before its official acceptance in Northumbria, and about sixty years earlier than
the north of Ireland. For Ireland we are fortunate in
possessing some of the literature of both sides of the
controversy, whereas for Wales we have only the picture
as it appears from the Anglo-Roman point of view. In
Bede's account of the controversy in Ireland, unlike
that with Wales, he closely follows official Canterbury
documents, and in addition to the letter from Laurentius of Canterbury just referred to, he gives us extracts
from two letters written from the popes to the Irish on
this matter. The first,[1] from Pope Honorius, *c.* 634, urges
them 'not to think their small number on the utmost

[1] Ibid. ii. 19.

edge of the earth'[1]—again the old phrase—'wiser than all the ancient and modern Churches of Christ throughout the World',[2] and not to celebrate Easter contrary to 'the Paschal calculation and decrees of all the bishops upon earth'.

From the letter written by Cummian (cf. p. 125),[3] thought to be probably abbot of Durrow, to Segéne, bishop of Iona (623-52), it seems that a considerable body in the south-east of Ireland were by this time in favour of full conformity with the continental usage, and as early as 629 most of this area had already celebrated Easter according to Roman practice. The letter is thought to have been written c. 632-3. The text is imperfect, but the general tenor is clear. The writer states that he has made a careful study of the Roman dating of the Easter Cycle, and has consulted his elders,[4] the coarbs of certain monastic foundations. Of these he enuerates five who had assembled, either in person or by deputy, at Mag-Léna in Offaly near Durrow, where a synod had been held at which it seems the new order had been accepted. It is clear, however, that the synod did not represent the united opinion of the ecclesiastics of the south of Ireland. Controversy was rife, and Cummian adds that a reactionary movement had set in, claiming to adhere to the traditions of the fathers.[5] The

---

[1] In extremis terrae finibus.

[2] Plummer (Bede, ii. 112) points out that the Irish often speak of themselves as iarthar domain, 'the west, or hinderpart of the World'.

[3] The text of the letter is published in Migne, P.L. lxxxvii, cols. 969 ff. For some account of this letter see Kenney, op. cit., p. 220; cf. also C. W. Jones, op. cit, pp. 8 ff. See also more recently an article by J. E. L. Oulton, 'The Epistle of Cummian, De Controversia Pascali' in Studia Patristica, ii (Berlin, 1957), pp. 128 ff.

[4] 'Successores videlicet nostrorum patrum priorum'.

[5] 'Traditiones seniorum servare se simulans'.

leader is not named, but there would seem to be a reference to another synod[1] held in Mag-Ailbe on the borders of Kildare and Carlow, described as *magnum concilium populorum Hiberniae*, who, so Cummian claims, instead of unity created division.[2] In this dilemma the pro-Roman party sent an embassy to Rome for guidance, which returned with added authority from the Holy City, and in 636 we are told that the south of Ireland joined 'the new Order which had lately come from Rome'.[3] It is interesting to note the reference to direct communication between the south of Ireland and Rome at this early date.[4]

The north of Ireland showed no signs of conformity as yet. A letter from John, who succeeded Honorius, written in 640 while he was still Pope Elect, was addressed to Tomianus mac Ronáin, abbot and bishop of Armagh; Columbanus, abbot and bishop of Clonard; Cronán, bishop of Nendrum; and others. In this he explained the Easter computation and urged them to crush the revival of Pelagianism among them. During the rest of the century, however, two influences were at work towards unity. The first, operating from within Ireland itself, was the cult of St. Patrick, the development of the see of Armagh and of the conception of

[1] We have some account of this synod in the legendary *Life of St. Fintan or Munnu*, chs. 26 f. Plummer, *Vitae Sanctorum Hiberniae*, ii (Oxford, 1910), pp. 226 ff.

[2] 'Qui utrumque non fecit unum sed divisit'.

[3] 'Novus ordo qui nuper e Roma venit'.

[4] An account of the controversy and a detailed analysis of Cummian's letter is given in B. Mac Carthy's Introduction to the *Annals of Ulster*, iv, p. cxxxviii. For a more detailed discussion and fuller references, see *Studies in the Early British Church*, edited by N. K. Chadwick (Cambridge, 1958), pp. 51 ff. Kenney (loc. cit.) points out that this letter, if genuine, is the only important controversial document written in Ireland on the Paschal question. It also contains our earliest reference to St. Patrick.

the work and prestige of the saint himself. Perhaps the two most important documents which we possess representing this point of view are Muirchu's *Life of St. Patrick*, and Tírechán's *Memoir*, both composed towards the end of the seventh century, and both manifestly composed in the interests of the see of Armagh and of Patrick as the saint of Ireland.

This is made clear in Muirchu's *Life* by the stress on unity, and the prominence given to Patrick's first celebration of Easter; and in Tírechán's *Memoir* by the author's avowed purpose of making a formal record of the see of Armagh and Patrick's foundations. Both Muirchu himself and Aedh, bishop of Slétty, to whom Muirchu dedicates the *Life*, subscribed in 697 to conformity with the Roman Order,[1] probably at a Synod of Birr, to which I shall refer more fully presently. In a note in the *Book of Armagh* we read that 'Bishop Aed dwelt in Slébte. He went to Armagh. He brought a bequest to Segéne of Armagh (d. 688)...and...offered a bequest and his kindred and his church to Patrick till Doom.'

Then, in regard to Segéne's successor, Fland Feblae: 'Aed [of Slébte] left a bequest with Conchad. Conchad went to Armagh, and Fland Feblae gave his church to him and he took himself as abbot.'[2]

It is only right to add that in the writings of Muirchu and Tírechán, as in the contemporary literature of the Anchorites, the purpose is to defend and establish what had long been accepted without question—in the case of the two former writers St. Patrick's long connexion

---

[1] See J. B. Bury, *The Life of St. Patrick* (London, 1905), p. 261.
[2] See *The Book of Armagh*, edited by J. Gwynn (Dublin, 1913), p. 457.
[3] Loc. cit.

with the see of Armagh aud the wide importance of the latter—rather than to create new claims.[1]

It is to be suspected that important pressure may have been put on the north of Ireland directly from Whithorn[2] to join the Roman Order. We know from the evidence of tombstone inscriptions that an important early Christian settlement was in existence here already by the close of the Roman period, but we know nothing further till towards the close of the seventh century, when a bishopric of Whithorn was revived, or more probably created, with Pecthelm, a pupil of Aldhelm of Malmesbury, as its first bishop. Pecthelm was in correspondence with both Aldhelm and Bede. A *Life of St. Ninian* was composed about this time, probably under the auspices of Pecthelm himself, and a couple of poems are extant which were composed in the following century relating to the same saint. It is from the

[1] The point is rightly stressed by Seán Mac Airt in *Saint Patrick*, edited by the Rev. John Ryan, S.J. (Dublin, 1958), p. 69.

[2] Much archaeological effort and place-name speculation has been expended in an attempt to account satisfactorily for the name *Candida Casa*, which from its Anglo-Saxon form has survived in the modern *Whithorn*. The excavation of this early site, although of great interest in itself, can give no clue to the name, which Bede himself has explained quite satisfactorily: 'Because it was built of stone which was unusual among the Britons'. Rough stone monuments have at all times been common in Scotland. What undoubtedly constituted the striking feature of *Candida Casa* was its church, traditionally built of stone, like the early Saxon churches of Northumbria. The colour, whether dark or light, is of no consequence. As dressed stone it would shine in sunlight and as such be distinctive in a country where wooden buildings were the rule. Exact parallels are the name of the Yugoslav capital Belgrade (*Beograd* from *Belo-grad*, 'white city'), and in Russia the traditional epithet of Moscow, which is invariably referred to in oral poetry as either *granovitaya Moskva*, 'Moscow of the rusticated (faceted) walls', or still more often, *Belo-kamennaya Moskva*, 'Moscow of the white stone walls', both having reference to the dressed stones of the walls of the Kremlin, striking to the eye accustomed to the wooden buildings of Russia.

information supplied to Bede by Pecthelm that Bede obtained the brief note on St. Ninian[1] which he has left us, and these late documents constitute, in fact, the only information that we possess about the saint except the work of Aelred of Rievaulx which is much later and quite unreliable. The concentration of the best literary elements interested in the Roman question on this remote outpost of Galloway is best accounted for by regarding it as in fact an advance post, a spear-head, for mission work in Ireland on this all-important question. Pecthelm is to be regarded as the spokesman of the element in the Church represented by Aldhelm and Bede.

It was desirable to have St. Ninian, the apostle to the southern Picts, of whatever date, in the picture, in view of the signature of Bruide mac Derile (d. 706), king of the southern Picts, at the Synod of Birr, and of the mission of Nechtan, his brother and successor as king of the southern Picts, to Bede's abbot Ceolfrith of Jarrow shortly before 717. The coincidence of the entry of these two kings of the southern Picts into the *unitas catholica* with our first information about their first missionary Ninian, the creation of his legend and the new bishopric at Candida Casa, and the names of the first two bishops, *Pect-helm*, 'Guardian of the Picts', and *Pect-wine*, 'Friend of the Picts', is perhaps best explained by the ecclesiastical politics of the time.[2] In fact we may

[1] I have offered some detailed considerations of our sources for knowledge of St. Ninian in 'St. Ninian: A Preliminary Study of Sources', *Transactions and Journal of Proceedings of the Dumfriesshire and Galloway Natural History and Antiquarian Society*, xxvii (1950).

[2] These names are not confined to the Whithorn tradition, however, but are common also in the Durham *Liber Vitae*; I am indebted to Mr. John McQueen who called them to my notice.

regard the first external influence operating on Northern Ireland as that of Malmesbury (through Pecthelm), whose great Abbot Aldhelm was a devoted pupil and disciple of the Canterbury school.

Perhaps the most general external pressure brought to bear strongly on the north of Ireland is the direct intervention of the Church in Northumbria, which had officially abandoned the Celtic for the Roman Order at the Synod of Whitby in 663. English noblemen had been in the habit of resorting to Ireland for purposes of study. Among them was the monk Ecgberht, who spent the greater part of his long life in seeking to win over the north of Ireland to Catholic unity, and who had become the chief representative of the Anglo-Roman party in the country. Towards the close of the century (c. 697 A.U.) he was joined in this work by Adamnán, the learned abbot of Iona.[1] During 686 and the two following years Adamnán had been absent from his *familia* on Iona and staying at the court of his *amicus*, his royal *alumnus*, 'pupil' Aldfrith, in Northumbria. Bede tells us specifically that he had been sent by his people to make careful inquiries into the Easter question, and that while there he had become convinced of the soundness of the reform;[2] but he was unable to persuade the community of Iona to accept the Roman canonical rites.[3] Thereupon he sailed to Ireland, and, so Bede assures us,[4] 'brought almost all that were not under the organisation of Iona[5] into Catholic unity'.

[1] The part played by Adamnán is fully set forth by Bede, *H.E.* v. 15.
[2] Ibid. 21.
[3] See the *Three Fragments of Annals* (edited and translated by J. O'Donovan (Dublin, 1860), pp. 110–14.
[4] *H.E.* v. 15.   [5] *qui ab Hiensium dominio erant liberi.*

The Synod of Birr is commonly known as 'Adam-nán's Synod', and is regarded as the official acceptance of the Roman Order in the north of Ireland. The event may probably be dated in 696.

Bede never gives us any hint as to the centre from which Ecgberht and Adamnán carried on their protracted negotiations in Ireland. After the Synod of Whitby in 663 Colmán, we are told by Bede, following upon a brief intermediate sojourn on Iona and a further sojourn on the Island of Inishbófin off the Mayo coast, left his Celtic followers on the island, but established his Saxon followers in a monastery which he founded specially for them in Mayo on the mainland. Bede reports that in his own day it was still occupied by English monks and had grown very large and had a reformed constitution[1]—by which Bede undoubtedly means it had accepted the Roman Order. From Alcuin later, and from a number of Irish sources, including annals, we know that the monastery was known as *Mag-n-Eo na Sachsan*, 'Mayo of the Saxons', and that it had a distinguished career, lasting at least till the fifteenth century. A Saxon community in the heart of western Ireland could hardly have thriven thus unless it fulfilled some important function. A possible explanation which occurs to me is that from the time of Ecgberht and Adamnán onwards, indeed from the time of Colmán, or shortly after, Mayo of the Saxons formed the headquarters of the Anglo-Roman party in northern Ireland and kept in continual touch with Northumbria and York, as it is known to have done.

---

[1] For the organization of the Columban monasteries, see Plummer, *Baedae Hist. Eccles.* ii. 134 f.

Bede tells us that after Adamnán's success in winning over northern Ireland to the *unitas catholica* he returned to Iona and died before he could win over his own community. But the ranks were closing in. In 713, while Bede must have been living at Jarrow as a young man, the famous Mission came to Abbot Ceolfrith from Nechtan IV, king of the southern Picts, and the Irish annals tell us that in 716 'the clergy of Iona were expelled by king Nechtan across Druim Alban'.

But on returning to Iona they found that the English monk Ecgberht had gone over to Iona[1] after the Synod of Birr, and two years later Iona celebrated Easter according to the Roman dating. But the prestige of Iona was gone. The supremacy of the Irish Church now rested in Armagh, and the chief authority of the Columban confederation eventually passed to Kells in Ireland and to Dunkeld in Scotland. Bede, writing shortly before 733, already speaks of Iona as a thing of the past.[2]

In Wales the change came surprisingly late, in North Wales not until at least a generation after Bede's death, and perhaps later in the south; in Devon and Cornwall not till the tenth century. The influence of Aldhelm of Malmesbury was exercised at an early date to bring them into the *unitas catholica*; yet over a century later King Ecgberht granted three estates to the Saxon bishop of Sherborne that 'from them he might year by year visit the Cornish people in order to extirpate their errors. For in time past they resisted the truth as much as they might.'[3] It was not till the time of Athelstan's conquest of Cornwall that the British bishop Conan

[1] Ibid. v. 22.
[2] Cf. Plummer, *Baedae Hist. Eccles.* ii. 135.
[3] See G. H. Doble, *Saint Gerent* (Shipston-on-Stour, 1938), p. 13.

K

submitted to Archbishop Wulfstan, and Aethelstan formally nominated him to the see of Bodmin in 936.

The Continent, as one might expect, was ahead of
Britain. Spanish Galicia had already accepted the reformed Easter at the Council of Toledo in 633 and in
the many Celtic monastic foundations in central Europe
the change had been largely effected by the eighth century. Louis the Pious addressed an order to Matmonoth,
abbot of Landévénec, in the Crozon Peninsula of Brittany in 818, enjoining on the Breton clergy the abandonment of Celtic practices and the adoption of the Roman
tonsure and the Rule of St. Benedict; but nevertheless, as
one would expect, Celtic customs continued till very late.[1]

The change was a gradual one. The co-arbship was
the most characteristic of the Celtic institutions, by
which, as we have seen (p. 63 above), the bishopric
or abbacy[2] continued as a family property and inheritance.[3] This lasted for centuries. In Brittany it was
general till the legislation of a council in 1127.

Gerald of Wales has some horrific stories to tell us of
the working of the co-arbship in west Wales, at Llanbadarn Fawr, at the time of his visit in the train of
Archbishop Baldwin as late as 1188.

This church, like many others in Ireland and Wales, has
a lay abbot; for a bad custom has grown up among the
clergy of appointing the powerful people of a diocese as
stewards, or rather patrons and guardians of the churches;
who ... have usurped the whole right, leaving the clergy only
the altars with their tithes and oblations, and assigning even

[1] Cf. Kenney, op. cit., p. 173; Gougaud, op. cit., pp. 416 ff.

[2] Cf. Kenney, pp. 292, 353.

[3] On this subject see J. Conway Davies, *Episcopal Acts relating to the
Welsh Dioceses*, ii (1948), Introduction, p. 460.

these to their sons and relations in the church. Such defenders, or rather destroyers, of the churches have caused themselves to be called abbots. . . . We found . . . in the church of Llanbadarn . . . a certain old man, hardened in his sins, acting as abbot, and his sons officiating at the altar.

And Gerald goes on to give a startling picture of the same church on the authority of a Breton knight who had visited it in King Stephen's reign:

On a certain feast day, [says Gerald,] whilst both the clergy and people were waiting for the arrival of the abbot to celebrate mass, he perceived a body of about twenty young men, armed, according to the custom of their country, approaching towards the church; and on enquiring which of them was the abbot, they pointed out to him a man walking in front, carrying a long spear. Gazing on him and wondering, he asked if the abbot had not another garb, or a different staff, from that which he now carried before him. They answered 'No'. He replied: 'I have indeed seen and heard this day a strange marvel.'[1]

The celibacy of the clergy was one of the latest reforms to be introduced. In Wales the *clas* or monastic system was organized on a family basis. The members were related and married, and membership was hereditary, and the wives were also members.[2] Even after the Norman Conquest, when the *clas* developed into the chapter in the cathedrals, the clergy and the members of the *clas* refused celibacy, and the laity refused to observe the long list of marriages within the prohibited degrees till the Reformation. Both Lanfranc and Anselm

[1] *Itinerary through Wales*, Book II, cap. 4.
[2] For the two outstanding cases in which the history of a *clas* in Wales is traced, see Conway Davies, *Episcopal Acts*, ii. 493 ff. The two instances are Llanbadarn in Cardiganshire and Llancarfan in Glamorgan.

were constrained to write letters to Ireland protesting against marriages inside prohibited degrees, chiefly with stepmothers and sisters-in-law.

In Scotland even the reforms of the Church instituted by King Malcolm Canmore and his Saxon queen Margaret towards the close of the eleventh century made no attempt to abolish the co-arbship, or the filling of high offices in the Church by laymen, or the appropriation of the benefices of the clergy by the laity, and their being made hereditary in their families. Skene (writing in 1887) suggests in a picturesque passage that:

Possibly Queen Margaret was restrained by the knowledge that the royal house into which she had married owed its origin to the lay abbots of one of the principal monasteries, and was largely endowed with the possessions of the Church; and if in the council her eye lighted on her young son Ethelred, who, even in boyhood, was lay abbot of Dunkeld, her utterances on that subject could hardly be otherwise than checked.[1]

The controversy had been a dignified one on both sides. We hear no word of persecution, and the issue was fought out on intellectual lines. While the arguments tended to centre on points of detail which today seem to have less significance, these are in reality the symbols of the greater questions of conformity and unity which were the real issues. The fundamental principles were wider. The fundamental principle to which the Celtic people clung everywhere was their own ecclesiastical tradition. The Welsh and the West Britons were keenly alive to the danger of placing themselves under a neighbouring Saxon, or at least an Anglo-Roman,

[1] Skene, *Celtic Scotland*, ii. 350.

archbishop. His home was among the powerful Saxons whom the Celtic ecclesiastics must have regarded as parvenus in religion. They kept clear of the whole controversy, and maintained complete isolation in their mountains till a late date. But the result is that from Wales we have practically no literature that can be certainly dated to this period.

In Ireland, on the contrary, much of the earliest ecclesiastical literature undoubtedly owed its origin, directly or indirectly, to this controversy. The earlier age, the Age of the Saints and Anchorites and hermits of the sixth century, had no need to formulate its beliefs, its rules, and its penitential system, or to write its saintly biographies. These things were all a matter of received discipline, of common knowledge, and general acceptance. It is not accepted practice but opposition which stimulates a declaration, and the Irish Church in face of the challenge from Rome had need to define its position. A new situation had arisen as a result of the Roman challenge. A 'literature of the subject' was needed by the 'case for the defence', both for the information of the adherents of their own party, and also for propaganda against the Romanizing party, which was felt to be threatening cherished traditional usages with annihilation.

But the 'literature of the subject' does not embody a new system of thought. It contains nothing which is not directly derived from the Age of the Saints. What is new is the writing down and circulation of the traditions, both narrative and precept. It must have been abundantly apparent to the adherents of the Celtic Order that their oral precepts, their intimate little anecdotes of their saintly founders, their practical rules, could not stand against the newly introduced written authoritative works rapidly being produced by the Roman Church. The oral traditions of sixth- and seventh-century Ireland must be given the authority and prestige of written texts, which would be at hand for reference and for circulation, no longer subject to the endless variation of oral tradition. The Irish monastic Church was stimulated to substitute the written for the oral—eyes for ears. It is thus that I would interpret the nickname of the two monasteries on the two banks of the Liffey, Tallaght and Finglas, the 'Two Eyes of Ireland'. It is Tallaght that during the eighth century led the literary movement for the recording and formulating of much of the 'Literature' of this period.

It is thus also that I would account for the great output of religious literature of the seventh and eighth centuries, and a great increase of the professional writer and copyist, whose obits appear very often in the annals of this period. It is not a period of original thought, for it echoes and develops the thought of the Age of the Saints and Anchorites of the preceding century. It is a period of consolidation and organization, of the mobilizing of the intellectual specialists, the Anchorites of the monastic Church, and an implementing of their teaching by the scribes. It is not an Age of Reform, but of Formulation. It is as an element of this formulation that I would interpret the notice in the *Annals of Ulster*, (s.a. 780) of a congress of the synods in the *oppidum* of Tara attended by anchorites and scribes under the presidency of Duiblitir. Now Duiblitir was abbot of Finglas, one of the 'Two Eyes of Ireland', and Dr. Flower believed that this meeting of the anchorites and scribes at Tara, under the presidency of Duiblitir, 'Black Letter', 'Ink writing',[1] had as its object the writing down of rules and other anchorite literature. Writing was still a rare and impressive thing. They called the president of the Congress Duiblitir, 'Black Letter', 'Old Inky'; and his monastery and the other 'writing' monastery, Tallaght, the 'Two Eyes of Ireland'.

The name of Máelrúain, the other 'Eye of Ireland', the 'opposite number to "Black Letter" (Dublitir)', is associated with some of the most important religious literature of the period; and almost all the literature of his School is of a personal character. Martyrologies, Rules, and Penitentials are among the most numerous texts, but the *Stowe missal*[2] is ascribed to the same school. A valuable source of information to after ages is the *Félire* or *Martyrology* composed by Oengus the Culdee evidently in the tradition of Tallaght (cf. p. 88 above), since the latest saint commemorated in it is the author's *aite*, or tutor, Máelrúain (d. 792). Most of the saints are Irish and, as Kenney observes, 'The work is indeed a witness to the unified national character of the Old Irish Church.'[3] It reads somewhat like a concise dic-

---

[1] A medieval Irish poem speaks thus of writing on the white vellum:
> My little dripping pen travels
> across the plain of shining books (i.e. white vellum). . . .
> On the page it squirts its draught
> of ink of the green-skinned holly.
>
> (Kuno Meyer, *Ancient Irish Poetry*, p. 89)

[2] Kenney, pp. 692 ff.

[3] Kenney, pp. 480 f. The work is also known incorrectly as the *Martyrology of Tallaght*; but the latter work was, in fact, a calendar of saints probably prepared at Tallaght in the eighth century. This Latin *Martyrology* has been shown to be the basis for the Irish *Martyrology of Oengus* to which some later additions were made. *The Martyrology of Tallaght* is edited by R. I. Best and H. J. Lawlor (London, 1931).

tionary of Irish saints, the original part being in verse, the later commentaries in prose. It is, in fact, a personal document in the fullest sense.

In the first half of the ninth century a monk, believed to have been one of the community of Tallaght, wrote down the traditions of the teaching and precepts of Máelrúain, which he had received, not directly from Máelrúain himself, but from Máeldithruib, abbot of Terryglas on Lough Derg in Co. Roscommon. With these *memorabilia* he has included in his dossier some additional precepts derived from the Rule and the Penitential composed in the Tallaght School and also some delightful little illustrative anecdotes. It is a curious and fascinating document,[1] a kind of commonplace book of the beliefs and practices of a little community, the sayings of Máeldithruib, abbot of Terryglas. We might describe it as the notes of a monastic Boswell, whose Dr. Johnson was Máeldithruib himself. But although writing in all probability at Terryglas, the author is concerned not primarily with Terryglas but with the rules and customs of Tallaght as established by Máelrúain and transmitted by Máeldithruib. The document is, in fact, neither a memoir of Máelrúain nor a Rule of Tallaght, but something of both. No other monastic document of this early period conveys so intimate an impression of the kind of monastic teaching of the Anchorite School— the way in which monastic discipline was inculcated, how the teaching of the leaders of a monastic movement was conveyed by oral tradition, the methods of instruc-

[1] It is edited and translated by E. J. Gwynn and W. J. Purton, 'The Monastery of Tallaght' (*Proceedings of the Royal Irish Academy*, xxix (1911); and another recension under the title of 'The Rule of Tallaght' in *Hermathena*, xliv (1927). Cf. further Kenney, op. cit., p. 471.

tion, the mingling of precept with illustration and memorable anecdote. I have already referred (p. 89 above) to Máelrúain's stern rejection of the well-meant offer of Cornán, the Anchorite of Desert Laigen, to play the pipes and make secular music for him. This little document reads like the notebook of an advanced pupil among Máeldithruib's monastic disciples, or perhaps the handbook of his novice-master. It transports us directly into a little Irish ascetic community of the eighth century, and breathes the atmosphere of its schoolroom or novitiate. Its very formlessness is eloquent.

Máelrúain comes before us as a very life-like figure, and an inexorable disciplinarian. It is evidently the intention of the writer to represent his monastery as of a more ascetic discipline than that of the monastery of Duiblitir across the Liffey—Duiblitir, who had taken the chair at the synod of the *oppidum* of Tara—for in chapter 40 of this little document we are told that:

Dublitir came to Máelrúain urging him to give the brethren leave to drink ale on the three chief festivals in the year. Máelrúain replied: 'So long as they are under my control and keep my commands, they shall drink no drop that causes them to forget God in this place.'

'My monks drink ale', said Dublitir, 'and they shall be in the kingdom of God along with thine.' .

'I do not know about that', said Máelrúain; 'but this I know,' said he, 'every monk of mine that hearkens to me and keeps my Rule shall have no need of judgment to be passed on him, nor of the fire of Doomsday to cleanse him, because they shall be clean already. Not so thy monks; they shall have somewhat that the fire of Doomsday must cleanse.'

It is natural that in an ascetic Anchorite milieu almost all the literature dating from this period should be of a disciplinary nature, whether personal discipline or regular. Theology or religious speculation is practically absent, for the Faith had never been called in question in the Celtic Church. Its basis is assumed. The literature is largely penitential in character, composed for religious recluses by their leaders to guide them in their personal religious observances. We need not wonder if in the process the austerities have been heightened. Most of the Irish monastic Rules are believed to have been composed in the eighth and ninth centuries, though the Rule of Columbanus is probably his own composition and dates substantially from the sixth century. In general, however, the Rules derive their material from the oral traditions of the practices ascribed to the saints whose names they bear, e.g. Ailbe of Emly-Íbhar in east-central Munster; Mochuta of Rathen and of Lismore in Munster; Ciarán of Clonmacnoise in the west on the Shannon; Columcille in Iona, &c. These Rules relate to personal austerities, and are obviously designed for ascetics.

The earliest of the Rules, which has been preserved in the original Irish text, is a brief prose work commonly called the *Rule of Columcille* (*Incipit regula Colaim Cille*);[1] but it is believed to be a prose paraphrase of a verse Rule by Máelrúain. This is the true Rule of the Culdees, and breathes the very spirit of the Anchorites, and the sweetness and gentleness of a faith so fresh, a contemplative Order so lofty, that monastic regulations and obedience hardly need a place here. The opening words at once speak of the personal responsibility of the individual for his spiritual life: 'Be alone in a place

---

[1] For the text see Kuno Meyer, *Zeitschrift für celtische Philologie*, iii. 28 f.; and for the text and translation see Haddan and Stubbs, *Councils*, ii, i. 119 f.

apart near a chief *lavra* (*catháir*)[1] if thou hast doubt in thy conscience about being in the company of many.'

The choice is between the coenobitic or 'monastic' and the anchoritic way of life, but here, as in the East, there is no opposition. The Anchorite, even if a recluse, will ordinarily be in touch with his community. The spirit which inspired St. Aidan and the brethren of Lindisfarne, and which won unstinting praise from Bede, breathes in this Rule of the Culdees:

Forgiveness from the heart to everyone.
Constant prayer for those who trouble thee.
Fervour in singing the office for the dead, as if every faithful dead were a particular friend of thine.

And this is important:

Three labours in the day, viz. prayers, work, and reading.

We are *en rapport* with the hermits of the East, the purity and loving-kindness of the Desert Fathers portrayed for us in the works of Cassian; and the importance of reading.

The personal nature of the literature of this period is very characteristic of the Penitentials. In these the sins are separately classified, and the appropriate penance for each type of sin is closely defined. The system of penance is extremely rigorous, and is largely responsible for the view sometimes held by modern scholars that the Irish Church was the most ascetic in the world. As a matter of fact the Irish austerities at their most severe cannot be compared with those of the Syrian saints.[2]

---

[1] i.e. a little monastic settlement.
[2] For example, in the ascetic discipline set forth by S. John Climacus in *The Ladder of Divine Ascent*. There is an English translation by the Archimandrite Lazarus Moore (London, 1959).

We have no serious evidence in the Celtic Church of stylites, like St. Symeon of Antioch,[1] or St. Daniel on the Bosphorus, no static saints, or saints in holes underground or cages, like St. Theodore of Sykeon.[2]

Yet the view commonly held that the austerities practised by the Celtic monks have exceeded those of other Christian countries (cf. p. 103 above) would perhaps not be wholly without justification if we were to regard the *Penitentials* as realistic documents based on practical experience. It would seem more probable, however, that many of their more extreme provisions are the outcome of the Irish love of casuistry and hypothetical legal analysis and theoretical cases. We may be sure that many of these cases are the webs spun in the casuistry of the monkish brain. They form an abstract compendium of suppositious crimes and unnatural sins, thought up in the cloister by the tortuous intellect of the clerical scribe, the disciplinarian searching overdiligently for every contingency that his casuistry can produce, so that nothing, however remote, may pass unprovided for. But the history of the Irish annals, the sweet and simple *Lives* of the early Irish saints of our

---

[1] See Nöldecke, *Sketches from Eastern History*, vii, 'Some Syrian Saints' (translated by J. S. Black, London and Edinburgh, 1892).

[2] See the Lives of 'St. Daniel the Stylite' and 'St. Theodore of Sykeon' in *Three Byzantine Saints*, translated from the Greek by Dawes and Baynes. It is not impossible that some so-called 'caves' or underground chambers (cf. p. 92 above) have their origin in such a custom. It is not easy otherwise to account for such earth-houses in Irish churchyards still surviving today, as, for example, at the cathedral church of Killala in north Mayo, and Kilcolumcille in Co. Donegal. Reference may be made also to the *souterrains* recorded in early monastic settlements of Illanloughan, Kildreelig, and Skellig Michael (all in Kerry) noted by F. Henry in her survey of *Early Monasteries*, &c., pp. 97, 110, 126 (and plate xix), ed. cit.

hagiographical traditions, above all their own poetry, tell a very different tale of the monkish life.

The penitential discipline had been a feature of increasing importance in the Continental Church from the third and fourth centuries, and was being progressively systematized. In monastic circles the leaders, who were careful students of Cassian, himself a deep student of Eastern monasticism, compiled their Penitentials on the graded system of the eight principal vices systematized in his writings. The great difference between the continental systems of penance and the Irish was that throughout the ancient period of the Continental Church penance was a public act, and its consequent reconciliation was regarded as a public rite, taking place in church before the congregation.[1] In the Celtic Church, on the other hand, as we have seen, private penance was privately imposed by a confessor (in Ireland *anmchara*,[2] 'soul-friend', in Wales *beriglour* or *periglour*)[3] and privately performed by the penitent; and this would seem to be a natural development in a Church

---

[1] J. T. McNeill and H. M. Gamer, *Medieval Handbooks of Penance* (New York, 1938), pp. 7, 13, 19. For a study of the system of penance in the Continental Church, see R. C. Mortimer, *The Origins of Private Penance in the Western Church* (Oxford, 1939). The author demonstrates the virtually exclusive recognition of the principle of public penance in the Continental Church down to the time of Gregory the Great, and ascribes the spread and ready acceptance of the principle of private penance to the Celtic and Anglo-Saxon missionaries. He argues, however, that the way was partly prepared in the fifth and sixth centuries by the growing emphasis on death-bed penance, and the consequent increasing responsibility of the parish priest.

[2] The saying 'Anyone without a soul-friend (*anmchara*) is like a body without a head' is attributed to both St. Brigit and St. Comgall in the *Martyrology of Oengus*, notes to 1 Feb. and 1 Aug. (4). See the edition by Whitley Stokes (London, 1905), pp. 65, 181 respectively.

[3] Possibly connected with the *oratio periculosa* of the Mass (Stokes); or with *parochiarius*. The word seems to be of Latin origin.

which was not an urban institution, and especially one in which eremitism was so important a feature. Indeed it is difficult to see how public penance could have been practised in the Age of the Saints. It is in fact believed that the emphasis on confession and works of penance is one of the features which differentiate the Irish monastic Church of the sixth and seventh centuries from the Continent; and that the Old Irish Penitentials, both in Latin and Irish, date from this period.[1] It is also claimed that the system of private confession and penance was eventually introduced into both the Anglo-Saxon and the Continental Church by Irish missionaries and their penitential books; but with this later development we are not here concerned.

The extent and the early date of Irish penitential compendia are among the most impressive features of her early literature. This is not the place for a detailed treatment of the penitential books, which is a vast and most intricate subject, but a word on the earliest Irish texts is relevant to our study. Among the earliest of these of which we hear is the *Penitentiale Venniani*, 'The Penitential of Finnian'. It is probably as early as the sixth century, and the author is probably the *Vennianus auctor* referred to by St. Columbanus in his letter to Gregory the Great as having consulted Gildas on

---

[1] See Kenney, op. cit., pp. 235 ff. The most important studies of the origin and character of the Irish penitentials are those of J. T. McNeill, 'The Celtic Penitentials', *Revue celtique*, xxxix (1922) and xl (1923); and of Mortimer, op. cit. The work of T. P. Oakley, *English Penitential Discipline and Anglo-Saxon Law* (New York, 1923), gives much attention to Irish and British sources, and refers to the latest critical scholarship. The fundamental lines of the study were laid down by F. W. H. Wasserschleben, *Die Bussordnungen der abendländischen Kirche* (Halle, 1851),

a point of monastic discipline (cf. p. 73 f. above). As Kenney points out,[1] the fact that the *Penitentiale Columbani* draws extensively on that of Vennianus makes this identification the more probable. The work of Vennianus deals with the sins of both clerics and laity, and has a special interest for us because it is mainly based on sources which are now lost. Vennianus shows no consciousness of originating a new tradition, and his work, like most of the literary works of the Irish Church of this period,[2] is probably mainly a codification of current practice among his associates. McNeill points out that Columbanus was a pupil in turn of two of the pupils of Finnian of Clonard, viz. Sinell and Comgall.

Columbanus himself is reported by his contemporary biographer Jonas to have made use of the penitential discipline, and according to McNeill already in his day, during the last ten years of the sixth century, the use of Celtic penitentials had become a Celtic custom. On the whole it would seem probable that he was the author of the *Penitentiale Columbani*, but that the work was written at different times, perhaps with the *Penitentiale Venniani* in mind, and perhaps never codified in a final form, or compiled with any attention to literary style—perhaps a working copy. The work enjoins confession 'to a priest', so we may perhaps suspect that here, as in the case of Columbanus's *Regula Coenobialis*, a certain amount of later interpolation has taken place in the text.[3]

[1] Kenney, p. 240, and see especially n. 250; McNeill and Gamer, *Medieval Handbooks of Penance*, p. 87.

[2] McNeill and Gamer, loc. cit.

[3] See G. S. M. Walker, *Sancti Columbani Opera* (Dublin, 1957), p. xliv. and further Dom Jean Laporte, *Le Pénitentiel de Saint Colomban* (Rome, 1958).

The only Penitential in the Old Irish language so far published[1] is believed to be at least as early as 800. It is a composite document derived from an archetype, and from earlier Penitentials, notably those of Theodore of Canterbury and of a certain Cummean, both of whom are mentioned by name. The latter is probably Cuimíne Fota, the great abbot of Clonfert, who died in 662.[2] The Old Irish text is also closely related to the *Penitentiale Bigotianum*, dating from the late seventh or early eighth century, and so called from the name of the *Codex Bigotianum 89* in Paris. The latter Penitential is of special interest, partly for the fact that it introduces in its preface commutations by which long penances may be altered to short and more severe ones, or commuted for money payments; and partly because, though the manuscript was written in Brittany or Normandy in the tenth or eleventh century, and the script is Continental, certain features, e.g. the abbreviations, give evidence that the document descends from an insular original, and the Codex which contains it is mainly a collection of insular materials. Gwynn and Kenney both regard it as earlier than the *Old Irish Penitential*.

The *Old Irish Penitential* has many individual features of special interest, however, such as the influence of the civil laws and authority, recognizable in the substitution of fines and compensation for ecclesiastical penalties, while in one passage the secular prince is recognized as having authority along with the bishop. The monastic purpose of the whole, however, can hardly be doubted.

---

[1] Published with text, translation, introduction, and commentary by E. J. Gwynn, *Ériu*, vii (1914). See also commentary by J. T. McNeill, *Revue celtique*, xxxix (1922), p. 298.

[2] His obit appears in the *Cambrian Annals*, s.a. 661.

We may point to the references to the 'church of the community', to the 'brethren', to the penalties of separation and exile, and to the insistence on the renunciation of personal property. As Gwynn observes, all this is in keeping with the monastic character of the early Irish Church and confirms the statement with which one manuscript of the text begins, that this *Penitential* was drawn up 'by the venerable men of Ireland'. Gwynn adds that although foreign models are used, they are adapted to the special conditions of the Irish Church.

It is only to be expected that a Church which has developed a form of eremitism so similar to that of Syria should have given attention to liturgical and hagiographical works. To the seventh century belongs the most ancient liturgical monument of the Irish Church, the *Antiphonary of Bangor*, which is believed to be probably of Irish origin, and which contains anonymous hymns of the fifth or sixth century. The manuscript tradition seems to be Irish.[1] Other works of general ecclesiastical importance for Ireland were also compiled at this time. One of the most important documents, believed to have been composed *c.* 700, is the *Collectio Canonum Hibernensis*, the collected canons of a number of Irish synods to which reference has been made above.

The most interesting of the literary developments of this period, however, and perhaps the one which had the most permanent influence on later literary development, is the *vita*, the narrative form of the *life* of a saint, as contrasted with the forms in which the traditions of the saint had previously been recorded. The earliest

[1] See Kenney, p. 261, where also references to translations, both in prose and verse, are given.

form of a saint's *life* is the commemorative sermon preached on the anniversary of his death, such as that preached by Hilary of Arles in commemoration of St. Honoratus, the founder of the monastery of the island of Lérins *c.* 410, and its abbot during Hilary's own early life on the foundation.[1] In this the main events of the saint's life are given in summary form. A later form of *vita* is that in which the principal *acta* of a saint are enumerated, not as narrative in chronological order, but in groups under certain headings. A fully developed example from the seventh century is *Adamnán's Life of St. Columba*, not in fact a straightforward narrative, but a work divided into three principal headings ('Books') enumerating in Book I the saint's Prophecies; in Book II his Miracles; in Book III his Visions. But the narrative type of *vita*, introduced into the West by St. Athanasius with his literary masterpiece, the *Life of St. Antony* the great pioneer of Egyptian monasticism, soon became the form universally adopted. This new literary genre had a flying start in Gaul, soon after its publication, by Sulpicius Severus's *Life of St. Martin*. The number of manuscripts in which this *Life of St. Martin* is found in Ireland testifies to its popularity. One copy is included in the Book of Armagh alongside Muirchu's *Life of St. Patrick* and other important Patrician documents collected here by Ferdomnach[2] (d. 846) in the early ninth century.

The fashion of writing narrative biographies soon spread to the Celtic countries, and *Adamnán's Life of*

---

[1] *Vita S. Hilarii Arelatensis* (Migne, *P.L.* l, col. 1226); more recently edited by S. Cavallin, *Vitae Sanctorum Honorati et Hilarii Episcoporum Arelatensium* (Lund, 1952).

[2] He was working under the supervision of the abbot of Armagh in 807.

St. Columba in the form of *Acta* in three sections was really already old-fashioned in style when it was written. Towards the middle of the seventh century we have the *Life* of St. Columbanus, monk and scholar, a *peregrinus* who founded several libraries and schools of learning on the Continent, a narrative written by Jonas, a monk who had entered Bobbio, Columbanus's own foundation, shortly after the death of the founder. Jonas himself was an Italian by birth; but we have reason to believe that *vitae* were being composed in Ireland already by the first half of the seventh century. An extant *Vita of St. Brigit of Kildare*, composed in the middle of the seventh century by one Cogitosus, the 'father' of Patrick's biographer Muirchu, at the request of the community of Kildare, claims to derive its miracles from an anonymous *vita* of the first half of the century, probably the work of Ailerán *Sapiens*, or *a n-ecna* (d. ? 665), the *fer legind* or 'lector' of Clonard, and a scholar in his own right. We also possess a *vita* of Monenna or Darerca, patron saint of the nunnery of Killeevy near Armagh, again derived from a lost *vita* of the first half of the seventh century, though our extant eleventh-century *vita* is by one Conchubranus, probably a cleric of Kildare. Kildare was evidently a literary centre, and may have introduced this narrative style into Ireland, since Muirchu mentions in the Preface to his *Vita of St. Patrick*, which belongs to the latter part of the seventh century, that he is composing in a new style after that of his 'father' Cogitosus. It may be added that the literary phraseology of Muirchu's *Vita of St. Patrick*, Cogitosus's *Vita of St. Brigit*, and the *Vita of St. Samson of Dol* in Brittany, possibly of the same period, show impressive resemblances. This common phraseology is thought to be derived from Cassian's *Collationes*, and Duine has suggested[1] that there may have been literary manuals for the use of monks composing *vitae*. It is interesting to note that the *Vita Anonyma* of St. Cuthbert of Lindisfarne was composed towards the close of the seventh century by a monk of Lindisfarne,[2] a Columban foundation. The biography was in fact now the most popular form of literature in the Celtic Church. Wales in this, as in other matters, was late in adopting the new fashion, but in her colony Brittany a number of *vitae* of Welsh saints date from the ninth century or earlier, due possibly to the influence of the Gallo-Roman Church.

These early Celtic *vitae* are valuable sources for the period, though they require to be used very critically. They are not entirely oral traditions, but learned works for their day, and the learning can be deceptive if we are not on our guard. The *Life of St. Columba* by Adamnán is by no means a spontaneous production derived exclusively from tradition, but built up to a very considerable degree on extracts from other literary works.[3] Duine[4] has detected in the *Vita of St. Samson* influences, not only of the Bible, but also of the writings of Gregory the Great, Sulpicius Severus, St. Jerome, and Cassian. The *vitae* were in fact works of learning, and the authors had libraries to hand.[5]

[1] *Revue celtique*, xxxv (1914), p. 299, n.

[2] B. Colgrave, *Two Lives of St. Cuthbert* (Cambridge, 1940), p. 12.

[3] See the important article by Gertrud Brüning, 'Adamnán's Vita Columbae und ihre Ableitungen', *Zeitschrift für celtische Philologie*, ii (1917), pp. 213 ff.; also published separately, Halle a. S., 1916.

[4] *Origines bretonnes, Études des sources—Questions d'hagiographie et vie de S. Samson* (Paris, 1914), pp. 26 ff.

[5] See a valuable study of the literary relations of our earliest *vitae* by B. Colgrave, 'The Earliest Saints' Lives written in England' (*Proceedings of the British Academy*, xliv (1958)).

Not all the literature of the Age of the Saints had it birth in the south, e.g. in Munster, or in the east at Kildare in Leinster. Reference has already been made to the *Antiphonary of Bangor*, which contains the earliest anonymous hymns. From Bangor also came the great Columbanus with his monastic Rule and his Penitential. Perhaps the most interesting of the early literary figures of the north is Cennfaelad, poet, scholar, and grammarian,[1] who had his 'brain of forgetfulness' taken from his head after the Battle of Moyra, the battle in which Suibhne Geilt became *geilt*, a 'Grazer'. In less picturesque diction tradition relates that Cennfaelad (d. 675) had a head wound cured in a native monastic school where he was taught writing; and all the stories and poems recited to him he wrote down, and became the earliest writer of historical traditions on record. It is a typical Irish story of a *fili*, a man of the native learned class and a poet, becoming a *fer legind*, 'a man who read and wrote'.[2]

From the north also we have the records of the Irish heathen world of magic. In our study of the early Celtic Church it is easy to overlook the enormous wealth of oral tradition current in Ireland at this time. The amount of knowledge which the monks derived by listening to native learning, oral history, poetry, stories of magic and of the heathen gods was infinitely greater than what they learned from reading Latin books. In the seventh century a corpus of native heathen lore and

[1] He is said to be heavily indebted to Isidore of Seville. See G. Calder, *Auraicept na n-Éces*, p. xxxi.

[2] For a full-scale study of Cennfaelad and his importance for historical matter in the early annals, see the article devoted to him by Eóin McNéill, 'A Pioneer of Nations', *Studies*, iv (1922), pp. 13 ff. Cf. also Calder, op. cit., pp. xxvii ff.

literature of great charm was transcribed in the little monastery of Drumsnat in Co. Monaghan in the north and formed the contents of the earliest Irish manuscript of which we know the contents—the *Cín Droma Snechtai*.[1] It contained heathen stories and poems of the god Midir, who carried off the queen of the prehistoric king Eochaid; of the voyage of Bran to the Land of Promise over the ocean; of the god Manannán mac Lír from over the sea, and of how he became the father of the historical king Mongán[2] whose kingdom was in Antrim in Northern Ireland. A whole cycle of magical and heathen stories circle around Mongán, and have been preserved for us by the monks who wrote down early in the eighth century this collection of stories and poems from traditions of the seventh century and earlier.

This wealth of heathen supernatural associations of a seventh-century historical king is difficult to account for, and it has sometimes been suggested that possibly a heathen revival took place in Antrim at this time. Is it perhaps a protest against the levelling intellectual influence of the Roman Church? It can surely be no accident that these heathen traditions are the earliest to be written down and must have been handed direct from the Age of the Saints; but indeed the Irish monastic Church never turned a cold shoulder on its ancient secular traditions, but lovingly collected them in great vellum books, so large that they are almost libraries themselves. This, however, was much later. This *Cín*

---

[1] For the *Cín Droma Snechtai* see R. Thurneysen, *Die irische Helden- und Königsage bis zum siebzehnten Jahrhundert* (Halle a. S., 1921), pp. 16 ff.; G. Murphy, *Ériu*, xvi (1952), pp. 145 ff.

[2] His obit is entered in the *Annals of Ulster* in 624 (recte 625).

Droma Snechtai[1] must have been a little manuscript like the *Book of Durrow*, and its contents were evidently in oral circulation in the seventh century.[2]

Almost all the forms of literature for which Ireland was famous later originate in the period which we have been studying. The Irish annals begin to be contemporary in the seventh or early eighth century. There can be little doubt that the lyrical poetry, with its passionate defence of the Anchorite life, its emphasis on writing, and above all its devotion to simplicity and austerity, and its ever-recurring reference to nature and the wild things of the country, is conditioned and immediately stimulated, despite its sweetness and spontaneity, by the impulse to defend the free life of the Celtic monks among these things against the encroachment of a Church governed by law and order and a centralized foreign official authority. I believe that much of the best Early Irish literature was inspired directly or indirectly by the Paschal controversy.

Again and again one returns to the question: what were the conditions under which all this literary activity took place? We know that libraries and *scriptoria* developed in monastic institutions later; but what of the Age of the Saints and the Anchorites of the early period? Did the monks own their books personally, like Mac-Conglinne, the seventh-century scholar of Armagh in the medieval burlesque of MacConglinne,[3] who set off

[1] The *cin* is defined by K. Meyer as 'a layer of parchment of five sheets, quire, book (from L. *quinum*)' (*Contributions to Irish Lexicography*, Halle a. S., 1906), s.v.   [2] Cf. G. Murphy, loc. cit.

[3] *The Vision of MacConglinne*, edited and translated by Kuno Meyer, (London, 1892). In this story, as in the *Buile Suibhne*, (cf. p. 105 ff. above), the medieval satirist has preserved for us by his burlesque the traditional customs of an earlier age.

from Armagh to Cork with his books in a satchel on his back to cure the king of gluttony? Or were there communal supplies of books in the monasteries? Probably both existed, but in very short supply. There cannot have been room for large collections of books, or generous facilities for writing.

This is how an Irish scribe looked upon his task of writing, as he has described it in a little poem written in the margin of a copy of Priscian's Latin grammar, in the first half of the ninth century:

> A hedge of trees surrounds me,
> A blackbird's lay sings to me;
> Above my lined booklet
> The trilling birds chant to me.
>
> In a grey mantle from the top of bushes
> The cuckoo sings:
> Verily—may the Lord shield me—
> Well do I write under the greenwood.[1]

And in a little poem traditionally ascribed to a poet who died in 665[2] we have a picture of the ideal monastery as he conceived it:

I wish, O Son of the living God, O ancient, eternal King,
For a hidden little hut in the wilderness that it may be my dwelling.
An all-grey lithe little lark to be by its side,
A clear pool to wash away sins through the grace of the Holy Spirit. . . .
A southern aspect for warmth, a little brook across its floor,
A choice land with many gracious gifts such as be good for every plant. . . .
A pleasant church and with the linen altar-cloth, a dwelling for God from Heaven;

---

[1] Kuno Meyer, *Ancient Irish Poetry*, p. 99.   [2] Id., *Ériu* i. 38.

Then, shining candles above the pure white Scriptures. . . .
This is the husbandry I would take, I would choose, and
   will not hide it:
Fragrant leek, hens, salmon, trout, bees.
Raiment and food enough for me from the King of fair fame,
And I to be sitting for a while praying to God in every
   place.[1]

Of all the literature of the Anchorites it is the poetry
which speaks to us today with an urgency and a beauty
against which there is no appeal. It is the personal expression of the spiritual happiness—I will not seek for
a more high-sounding word—the spiritual happiness of
the Anchorite himself. It is perhaps the most remarkable
aspect of this Western asceticism that in addition to the
formulation of ascetic Rules and Penitentials the same
movement should also have produced a literature in
which the individual personality develops and becomes
articulate. Of all the early peoples in our islands these
scholars and ascetics were the first to speak in the first
person to us today, and the contact seems immediate.
Is it because this is scholars' poetry—and all scholars,
children of the Classics, speak the same language?—I
mean, speak in the same kind of way? They understand
one another.

One of the list of Deadly Sins which we share today
with both the solitaries of the desert and the Celtic
Anchorite is the temptation to fall into *accidie*, which
John Cassian describes[2] with such a brilliant flash of

---

[1] Kuno Meyer, *Ancient Irish Poetry*, p. 93.

[2] *Institutes*, x. ii. The works of Cassian are edited in Migne, *P.L.* xlix,
cols. 53 ff.; and by M. Petschenig, *Johannis Cassiani Opera*, 2 vols.
(Vienna, 1886 and 1888), translated into English by E. C. S. Gibson
(Oxford, 1894).

insight and experience. It is the sense of futility and doubt, of the frustration which attacks the religious and the scholar alike at times, making him restless, helplessly seeking some fresh stimulus when the steady flow of inspiration runs dry.

When this has taken possession of some wretched soul [writes John Cassian], it produces horror of the place, distaste for his cell, and disdain and contempt for the brethren. . . . He praises other monasteries and those which are more remote . . . and . . . he paints the intercourse of the brethren there as. agreeable and full of spiritual life. On the other hand he says that all around him is harsh, and . . . that there is nothing edifying among the brethren who dwell in that monastery.

Then:

He gazes about him uneasily this way and that (or, as we should say today, 'He bites his pen') and sighs that none of the brethren come to see him, and keeps going in and out of his cell, and gazes up at the sun very often as if it did not set quickly enough. (*He is still biting his pen . . . or maybe his nails*). . . He supposes that no remedy can be found for such an attack except in visiting one or other of the brethren. . . . Then the same malady suggests that visits are honourable and necessary duties, and should be paid to the brethren.

How familiar we all are with this mood in our less fruitful and happy hours!

The monk who wrote in some Irish monastery in the tenth century on the trouble which he had in keeping his thoughts in check is struggling with the same weakness as Cassian's solitary and ourselves.

Shame to my thoughts, how they stray from me!
I fear great danger from it on the day of eternal Doom.
During the psalms they wander on a path that is not right:
They fash, they fret, they misbehave before the eyes of
    great God. . . .
Neither sword-edge nor crack of whip will keep them down
    strongly:
As slippery as an eel's tail they glide out of my grasp. . . .
Rule this heart of mine, O dread God of the elements,
That Thou mayst be my love, that I may do Thy will.[1]

Yet this little poem, despite its humour and lightness
of touch, has an ear attuned to the divine judgement
and the Day of Doom.

In the poetry of the Age of the Saints this warning note
is not prominent. Instead we find a serenity and a simplicity like that which St. John felt as he stroked the
partridge, for his pleasant relaxation, and so offended
the philosopher who thought he was being frivolous.
Two centuries earlier than the penitent little poem *On
the Flightiness of Thought* we get the wise and light-
hearted poem of the *Monk and his Pet Cat* which has by
now become a classic.

I and my white Pangur
Have each his special art:
His mind is set on hunting mice,
Mine is upon my special craft.

I love to rest—better than any fame!—
With close study at my little book;
White Pangur does not envy me:
He loves his childish play.

[1] Kuno Meyer, *Ancient Irish Poetry*, pp. 35 f.; *Ériu*, iii. 13.

When in our house we two are all alone—
A tale without tedium!
We have—sport never-ending!
Something to exercise our wit. . . .

He rejoices with quick leaps
When in his sharp claw sticks a mouse:
I too rejoice when I have grasped
A problem difficult and dearly loved.

Though we are thus at all times,
Neither hinders the other,
Each of us pleased with his own art
Amuses himself alone.

He is a master of the work
Which every day he does:
While I am at my own work
To bring difficulty to clearness.[1]

The disappearance of the Celtic Church was inevitable. The absence of central organization and control
precluded permanency; but no one can come to the
end without regret for the loss of something rare and
valuable. Even Máelrúain, with his stern rejection of
poor Cornán who wanted to make music for him; his
uncompromising refusal to allow his monks to drink ale,
even on feast days; and his cheerful relegation of the
monks of Duiblitir's monastery just across the Liffey to
the purging fire on the Day of Judgement, cannot rob
the Age of the Saints and Anchorites of the beauty of
their simple, disciplined life and their lofty ideals. Its
greatest and lasting value is expressed over and over

---

[1] Kuno Meyer, *Ancient Irish Poetry*, p. 83.

again in its poetry, which places purity of spirit and integrity of heart above all formal regulations.

The poetry associated with the early hermits expresses not so much the formal observances of the penitential discipline as the simplicity and integrity of the spiritual *élite*. Theirs is no selfish withdrawal, but the attainment of spiritual perfection by a life purified from material desires in simple communion with nature. Some of the most exquisite of the lyrics belong by ascription to this early period of the Saints, and all alike share in the singular purity of their inspiration.

It is the unworldliness of the Anchorite poetry which strikes us most forcibly today. In the little poem on the death of *Alexander the Great*:

> Four men stood by the grave of a man,
> The grave of Alexander the Proud: . . .
> Said the first man of them:
> 'Yesterday there were around the king
> The men of the world—a sad gathering!
> Though today he is alone.'[1]

As we enter Kildare from the west today we pass a tall rath, or native Irish fort, by the roadside. It is topped by a little grove of old trees which have no doubt helped to preserve it. Near by is a modern road sign giving the local name of the village, *Rathangan*, and one of the earliest of our Irish poems at once comes to mind. It recounts the ancient kings of the local dynasty of Kildare.

> *The Fort of Rathangan—*
> The fort over against the oak-wood,
> Once it was Bruidge's, it was Cathal's,

[1] Ibid., p. 96.

> It was Aed's, it was Ailill's,
> It was Conaing's, it was Cuilíne's,
> And it was Maeldúin's:
> The fort remains after each in his turn—
> And the kings asleep in the ground.[1]

The saints of the early Celtic Church have a special kind of immortality which is their peculiar and rare privilege. Asking nothing for themselves, seeking only to be forgotten by men, in a union with the divine Spirit, they are yet remembered with a devotion rarely accorded to small groups of religious 'on the edge of the habitable globe'. I have said nothing of the *peregrini* who carried their learning and their literary traditions to the Continent, and who, in an age hardly later than the one which we have been studying, founded schools of learning and libraries throughout Europe.[2] The Celtic peoples of our early period had no towns, no currency, and no large-scale industries or fleet. Their languages are difficult and known to relatively few scholars outside their own country. Their wealth lies in their spiritual and intellectual endowments, and their contribution to civilization will be more fully appreciated in the future when their history and the riches of their manuscript possessions become more widely known.

---

[1] Kuno Meyer, *Ancient Irish Poetry*, p. 93. Cf. *Hail Brigit, an Old Irish poem on the Hill of Allen*, edited and translated by Kuno Meyer (Dublin, 1962).

[2] E. S. Duckett, *The Wandering Saints*, contains valuable references to Irish learning and to Irish learned saints on the Continent. See especially chapters 7, 8, and 9.